Against All Odds

Enjoy all your
adventures !

Roger

Against All Odds

The Stories of 25 Remarkable Adventurers

ROGER BUNYAN

HAYLOFT

First published in Great Britain by Hayloft Publishing Ltd, 2019

A CIP catalogue record for this book is available from the British Library

ISBN 978-1-910237-47-2

Designed, printed and bound in the EU

Hayloft policy is to use papers that are natural, renewable and recyclable products and made from wood grown in sustainable forests. The logging and manufacturing processes are expected to conform to the environmental regulations of the country of origin.

This book was printed with the offset of carbon emissions and support for Forest Protection in Pará, Brazil.

Hayloft Publishing Ltd,
a company registered in England number 4802586
2 Staveley Mill Yard, Staveley, Kendal, LA8 9LR (registered office)
L'Ancien Presbytère, 21460 Corsaint, France (editorial office)

Email: books@hayloft.eu
Tel: + 44 (0)7971 352 473 or +33 (0)380 896 760
www.hayloft.eu

For my wife Jackie

For my daughter Fern

In memory of Nikolay Baydin

Kazimierz Nowak on his bike trip through Africa.

Contents

Foreword

As eager outdoor enthusiasts in the 21st century, we are incredibly lucky. We're blessed with excellent navigational tools, we are able to head to the high street to purchase lightweight, reliable gear that has been through years of rigorous development, and we have the vast resources of the internet and decades of guide books at our disposal.

That's not to say that adventure is easy in modern times, but the adventurers of yesteryear had it far more arduous and challenging, with no promise of success, nor a safety net to catch them if they failed. With that, it's quite remarkable that such impressive achievements were made.

Many of these achievements are recognised and celebrated today, with the likes of Edmund Hilary, Ranulph Fiennes and Ernest Shackleton among those most well known. The truth is, however, that there are dozens of fascinating stories of hardy, pioneering men and women venturing to all corners of this globe that have been forgotten.

But these incredible stories are overlooked no more thanks to Roger Bunyan. For years Roger has been discovering and researching these remarkable people for a series of articles for *Adventure Travel* magazine titled 'History's Heroes'. With each and every tale, I am amazed at the unbelievable feats of endurance, fortitude and bravery that Roger so scrupulously researches and retells.

In *Against All Odds*, Roger puts a spotlight on many of these adventurous souls, pulling together a collection of captivating stories that deserve recognition and celebration for decades to come.

Rob Slade, Editor of *Adventure Travel*

Introduction

This book is a celebration of 25 adventurers who achieved a whole range of breathtaking feats during a period spanning some 60 to 150 years ago. These men and women carried out their adventures in a variety of ways and across all regions of the globe. Those on the list include mountaineers, polar explorers, long distance walkers, cyclists, caving pioneers, people using vessels from ships to canoes, horse-riders, some who took to riding a camel, an elephant, and some who swam!

You might say it was a golden age of adventuring; all these people were being taken by an irresistible desire to go into the unknown. Some of these journeys were part of an expedition, some were completed in small groups, while others were individual in their nature. There are those within the 25 whose main aim was to be the first to achieve a specific task, others were simply placing themselves within a wider, more encompassing challenge. Some adventures were relatively short in length, while others lasted much longer, sometimes taking years or an entire lifetime to achieve. For some, it simply became a way of life.

Although these people might have chosen different ways to follow their dreams, there are however, certain similarities between them all. It was at a time when people had an increased knowledge about far flung locations and were being lured away to have a look for themselves. They too could make their discoveries, have their own journeys and actually peer over the horizon. Another commonality between them, is a 'derring-do' gene running within all their veins. To imagine the impossible, to think out-of-the-box and just have a go. In the majority of cases, there were no previous reports of similar adventures to refer to. So, checking if plans were in any way feasible, invariably, wasn't an option! Not like today, where we have a plethora of references to muse over before taking on adventurous undertakings.

These brave men and women simply made their own rules as they journeyed their incredible paths. They had but rudimentary equipment, basic clothing, a vague plan and non-existent back-up if things went wrong. However, with a phenomenal mass of determination and enthusiasm… they went forth.

I happened upon these extraordinary stories whilst writing short articles entitled 'History's Heroes' for the magazine *Adventure Travel*. Once I learnt of one utterly captivating adventurer, I would then happen upon another… and then another…

As I researched each individual story, I couldn't believe what I was discovering! What was even more shocking, as a life-long outdoor pursuits enthusiast, was that many of these tales of adventure, I had never come across before. And, asking around, many of my 'outdoor' friends hadn't heard of them either. So, due to my writing for *Adventure Travel*, I was given an opportunity to introduce the magazine's readers to these 'against all the odds' pioneers of adventure from yesteryear. And now, the magazine has kindly allowed me to put these extraordinary stories into a book, for which I thank them.

Warning! There might well be some of you who read about these adventures and may think that there is a lack of detail or clarity about some aspects of their stories. This is a fair comment. However, given the pioneering nature of many of their feats and journeys, during the period in history and locations their adventures took place, and the exceedingly dangerous circumstances they often found themselves in, there might well be a few gaps in the facts. Indeed, it must be remembered that these adventures took place some time ago, so evidence may have been lost.

In a few cases, some records might have been deliberately destroyed for their owners' safety. For some, adventurers who were writing reports for publication back in their home countries, editors may well have exaggerated aspects of their journeys, in order to create a little more sensationalism for the public. However, despite some of these question-marks, I believe there are enough hard facts and evidence to say for sure, that these 25 historical adventurers all achieved some truly amazing feats. Each and every one of them is to be celebrated and I simply applaud them in their derring-do.

I strongly believe that the stories belonging to these brave people need to be kept alive. There is a danger such endeavours might easily become lost and forgotten upon the dusty shelves of time. By having their tales included in this book will, hopefully, go some small way in keeping their memories and accomplishments alive.

Even more importantly, such stories might actually be inspirational for another wave of future adventurers. It might capture the young, or the middle aged or indeed those of maturing years amongst you. Reading such stories might just ignite that adventurous spark within. Before you realise it, you will be planning and completing your very own escapades.

That would be such a fitting legacy for these somewhat forgotten heroes of adventure, wouldn't it? Let the challenges commence!

Edward Whymper, photograph courtesy of Zermatt Tourismus.

Edward Whymper

Who was he?

Edward Whymper was a British mountaineer, explorer, artist and author. He was at the forefront of exploring and climbing the major peaks of the Alps in what had became known as the 'Golden Age of Mountaineering'. He also made important explorations of other regions of the world.

Early Life

Edward was born in London in 1840, the second child of a family of eleven. His father had a successful wood engraving business which provided the means for his family to enjoy a middle-class lifestyle. He went to school until he was fourteen, after which, he joined the family business. As the years ticked by, Edward steadily acquired the intricate skills required to turn wood-engravings into book illustrations. He also became quite gifted in the use of water-colour. In 1860, he was asked by a publisher to go to the Alps and produce sketches for a book about the great Alpine peaks.

Visits to the Alps

For Edward, this initial excursion into the Alps was of huge importance and literally changed his life. That summer he spent a total of 47 days walking around the Alps and covered almost 1,000 kilometres. He fell in love with the sheer beauty of the mountains, the valleys, the many natural wonders and the Alpine villages. Not only did he sketch the mountainous vistas he saw but also the human characters he came across. Edward possessed a great deal of stamina and strength as he hiked, scrambled, crossed glaciers and ascended passes and some of the lower peaks.

The sketches Edward produced received high praise from the

publisher, so he was commissioned for the following season as well. Whilst journeying around the Alps, Edward had not only become infatuated with the mountains, but had also become intrigued by those he had met who climbed them. He developed a desire to join the ranks of the mainly British adventurers, led by local guides, who were wanting to ascend the 140 or so highest peaks of over 3,600 metres in height.

Each summer there had been an increasing number of the well-healed aristocracy, academics and clergy who were going-off to the Alps as 'peak-baggers'. In 1854, after a British man named Alfred Wills had climbed an Alpine peak and then written an account of his experiences, the sport of 'mountaineering' had been launched. The period became known as the 'Golden Age of Mountaineering' where all the highest summits were gradually being conquered. Edward intended to be part of this elite group.

Full of youthful zest and ambition, he returned to the Alps in 1861. With a guide, he climbed his first high Alpine peak, Mont Pelvoux at 3,946 metres. Having never been at such an altitude before, this was a phenomenal performance, given Edward's lack of experience and the rudimentary equipment of the day. Brimming with confidence, he then made his way to the Matterhorn straddling Switzerland and Italy and made plans to ascend the unclimbed mountain. To scale this most iconic of mountains was considered to be the greatest of mountaineering prizes of the period. He secured the services of a guide from the village of Breuil, on the Italian side of the mountain. They made their way onto the lower part of the Matterhorn, but as the climbing difficulties increased, an altercation with his guide took place, after which, the trip was aborted.

On his return to Britain, he made plans for his next trip. Edward decided to design a new mountain tent which would be more suited to the rigours of high altitude weather conditions than the ones in use. His 'Whymper Tent' formed a basic design for mountain tents for the next 100 years. After just two visits to these magnificent mountains, Edward had not only grown in confidence,

The Whymper tent.

enough to tackle the most challenging of Alpine peaks, but was also designing new equipment.

In the summer of 1862, Edward had again returned to the bottom of the Matterhorn to launch another assault on the mountain. By now, it had become an obsession: he wanted to be the very first person to ascend this reputedly impregnable mountain. But once again, Edward and his party were forced back because of the poor conditions. However, his newly designed tent had worked well in the wild weather upon the mountain. Some time later, he tried finding guides for another outing up the Matterhorn, but none were available. So, Edward went up on his own. He carefully climbed to where he had left his tent during his previous attempt and decided to stay the night. As he sat alone upon the mountain, looking out of his tent he described his view:

'The sun was setting and its rosy rays, blending with the snowy

blue, had thrown a pale, pure violet as far as the eye could see…
As I sat in the door… the earth [became]… almost sublime… the
moon as it rose brought the hills… into sight… yet more magnificent…'

Overnight in the Alps.

The following morning, he continued upwards, before retreat-
ing – yet again, after the climbing became more difficult. Unfortunately, at one very precarious location during his descent, he
fell some 60 metres, bouncing many times in an uncontrollable
descent. He picked himself up and although he was bleeding
badly, Edward managed to continue climbing downwards. At one
point he lost consciousness, but eventually staggered into Breuil
with his many cuts and abrasions. Three days later, he was again
climbing back up the Matterhorn's ridge, but this time, with a
porter. Again, he tried climbing higher and once more, difficult
climbing conditions forced a retreat.

The following season in 1863, was somewhat plagued by unsuitable weather conditions for much climbing to be carried out. After another failed attempt was made on the Matterhorn, Edward did succeed in making a first ascent of the nearby Grand Tournalin. The following 1864 season began well with first ascents of the Pointe des Ecrins, Mont Dolent, Aiguille de Trélatête and the Aiguille D'Argentière. Unfortunately, on arriving in Zermatt for another try at the Matterhorn, Edward was forced to forshorten his season, due to work commitments back in London.

With fresh vigour, Edward returned to the Alps for the 1865 season. By now, he had become one of the most high-profile and talented British climbers travelling to these mountains each summer. His on-going tussle with the Matterhorn was well known throughout the Alpine world. After many unsuccessful attempts, his enthusiasm showed no sign of abating. The season began well with a first ascent of the Grand Cornier and an ascent of the Dente Blanche. After that came another attempt on the Matterhorn, his seventh, but on this occasion, it was further to the east of previous

Climbing in the Alps.

outings. Again, it ended abruptly due to the amount of falling rocks endangering his party's progress. Edward headed for the mountains around Mont Blanc where he made first ascents of the formidable Grand Jorasses and the Aiguille Verte. It was time to return to the village of Breuil. What unfolded next, is now part of mountaineering legend.

Conquered then calamity

On meeting with the guide Jean-Antoine Carrell, Edward was told he would be unable to accompany him on his next Matterhorn bid. However, Edward soon learnt that a secret plan had been hatched for Carrell to accompany an entirely Italian group on an attempt on the Matterhorn which would not include Edward. Feeling betrayed at the clandestine nature of Carrell's actions, he made haste to Zermatt. On arrival, he wanted to find a guide who was available for an assault on the mountain from the Swiss side. He learnt that two Britains, the Reverend Charles Hudson and his companion, Douglas Hadow, had hired Michel Croz as their guide to climb the Hornli Ridge of the Matterhorn. Edward was overjoyed at being invited to join their party.

The four climbers then met another group who were also planning an ascent. That group consisted of Lord Francis Douglas with his guides Peter Taugwalder and his son, also called Peter. The two groups decided to join forces, so making a party of seven. This had now turned into a race to the top, one party from the Italian side, the other from the Swiss.

Although the Hornli Ridge looks exceedingly imposing, it proved to be easier to climb than Edward's previous attempts. By the afternoon of the second day, Edward's party stood triumphantly upon the summit. On his eighth attempt, Edward had finally climbed the Matterhorn. He wrote: 'The slope eased off, at length we could be detached, and Croz and I, dashing away, ran a neck-and-neck race, which ended in a dead heat. At 1:40 pm the world was at our feet, and the Matterhorn was conquered. Hurrah!'

The successful climb to the summit of the Matterhorn. Image courtesy of Zermatt Tourismus.

Feeling elated, the conquering climbers spotted the Italian party far below. They stood shouting and waving at their opponents. Edward's group had climbed the unconquerable mountain and had beaten the Italians to the top. Unfortunately, tragedy struck as the group of seven climbers descended. Not far from the summit, Hadow's foot slipped and he fell, dragging Croz, Hudson and Lord Douglas with him. The thin rope holding the whole group together snapped, and the four fell down the mountainside to their deaths. Luckily, Edward and the two Taugwalders were on the other side of the broken rope, they hung on to the mountain and survived. In total disbelief at what had just happened, the three survivors somehow managed to get down. Triumph had turned so quickly into tragedy.

There was an enquiry into the accident where Taugwalder senior was criticised for using an old and weak rope between him and the four who fell. There was even talk as to whether the rope had been cut. However, after the official hearing, he was eventu-

The broken rope! Courtesy of Matterhorn Museum, Zermatt.

ally acquitted. But the whole incident had highlighted the dangers of mountaineering. The incident had put both the Matterhorn and Zermatt on the world map and brought notoriety to Edward Whymper and the others involved. There followed a great deal of criticism in the British press and even Queen Victoria asked if laws could be passed to make mountaineering illegal.

Edward was totally devastated. The catastrophe had put pay to his peak-bagging in the Alps. He wrote: 'Every night… I see my comrades… slipping on their backs, their arms outstretched, one after the other, in perfect distances… Yes, I shall always see them…'

By the autumn, he had returned to his father's business in London but could not forget the incident which continued to haunt him for the rest of his days.

Greenland, Ecuador and Canada

By 1867, Edward's adventurous spirit had taken a new direction. Following his boyhood dream of Arctic exploration, he planned to explore the interior of Greenland. Although his journey was hampered by a lack of supplies, he concluded that if the correct sledges were used, it would be possible to journey into the glacial interior of the vast island. Edward's trip was more than just an exploration of the island because he was also involved in scientific discovery. During the expedition he had managed to collect a variety of specimens for the British Museum. In 1872, Edward returned to Greenland again, in order to survey the coastline.

Over the next few years, Edward wrote a book about his adventures in the Alps entitled *Scrambles Amongst the Alps*. It included his account of the ascent of the Matterhorn and the aftermath. The book became a best seller for which he became well known throughout the world. However, Edward's urge to explore and have additional adventures wasn't at an end. In 1880, Edward organised an expedition to the Andes mountains of Ecuador in order to make several mountain ascents and to carry-out scientific research. He had moved on from purely peak-bagging. His chief guide for the trip was Jean-Antoine Carrel, who had led the Italian party during the race to the top of the Matterhorn. They were again friends. Louis Carrel, his cousin and fellow guide, also went with them.

Edward's main objective was to ascertain how the human body functions when it is at high altitude. The expedition was a success because, after completing a number of experiments, Edward concluded that at very high altitudes, the performance of climbers becomes more physically challenging. His party made the first ascent of Chimborazo at 6,268 metres, which they climbed twice during the expedition. They scaled another six high mountains for the very first time, all of which were over 4,500 metres high. They also spent the night on top of the volcano, Cotopaxi, which is 5,897 metres in height.

During several summers at the start of the 1900s, Edward visited Canada as a consultant for the Canadian Pacific Raiway Com-

The summit of Chimborazo in Ecuador.

pany, advising them on how they could develop their mountain centres. During his visits he made first ascents of Stanley Peak and Mount Whymper, which was named in his honour.

Later Life

During his later years Edward became a notable public speaker giving talks about his climbs in the Alps and his other expeditions. After so many years as a bachelor, he finally married when he was 66 years old. He

Edward Whymper.

married Edith Lewin who was 21 years of age and they had one daughter who they named Ethel. Sadly, the marriage soon became an unhappy union and only lasted four years. Edward continued to visit the Alps for more leisurely excursions in his later years. On a visit to Chamonix in the French Alps during 1911, Edward became ill and died alone in his hotel room.

It was the end of what had been a most incredible life where Edward Whymper had been involved in a number of pioneering mountain adventures. In particular, his determination to climb, what had become known as the most impenetrable of all the Alpine mountains to conquer, was extraordinary. Mountaineers agree that by climbing the Matterhorn he brought to a close the Golden Age of Mountaineering.

Isabella Bird

Who was she?

Isabella Bird was one of the foremost travellers of the late 1800s. Her somewhat unorthodox adventures to hitherto little known locations were extraordinary feats for any traveller of the period, not least for a woman restricted by Victorian convention. Although she suffered ill health for much of her life, she became most alive during her many foreign journeys. Her favoured method of travel was by horse, although she also used mules and elephants along with numerous other forms of transportation. Her adventures have been superbly documented by both her books and her photography and have informed, amazed and inspired many people through the years.

Early Life

Isabella was born in Yorkshire in 1831 and, as a child, she suffered from a number of ailments. She had an operation to remove a tumour from her spine but unfortunately, it was only a partial success. It was suggested she spend as much time as she could in the open air, as a consequence, she learnt how both to ride and row. In order to improve her health the family would spend their summers amidst the pure air of Scotland. In 1854 doctors recommended she should travel in order to improve her condition. So her father, a clergyman, gave her £100 to go wherever she wished. Isabella decided to visit the United States and Canada and the trip did appear to improve her physical condition. On her return, she wrote about her experiences, the first of many travel books.

Her first adventures

However, Isabella's real adventures began in 1872 when she journeyed to Australia and New Zealand. After an invigoratingly wild crossing of the Pacific aboard a ship, she stopped-off at Hawaii, then known as the Sandwich Islands. She began exploring the islands by horse, but instead of using her usual side-saddle, she took to riding astride the horse. This method of riding immediately helped relieve her back-pain which she had continually suffered from. Such a simple remedy now gave her the mobility she desired, enabling her to visit remote areas all across these volcanic Pacific islands. She travelled with a number of different people and stayed in a variety of peoples' homes along the way.

Highlights of her explorations were visits to various volcanic features. Isabella climbed the highest mountain on Hawaii, the dormant volcano of Moana Kea, at 4,207 metres. She also became only the second woman to ascend the active volcano of Mauna Loa, which rose to 4,160 metres. Isabella made these ascents with two local islanders and William Green, a British shipping agent and volcanologist. She crossed lava flows and ascended steep rocky terrain to gain the volcano's summit with its cold air and gases escaping out of fissures. The party camped on the very rim of the crater where they were in easy view of the flows of fiery molten rock coming from Mauna Loa. She wrote, 'Huddled up in blankets, we sat on the outer ledge in solemn silence to devote ourselves to the volcano.' They then viewed the mountain's firework display. After six months of travelling throughout the islands, it was time to move on.

Isabella Bird.

Next, Isabella sailed to the United States where she made her way to Colorado. There, she rode over 1,200 kilometres throughout the southern Rocky Mountains, across all kinds of terrain and in all weathers. At the time of her visit, this region of the mountains was considered lawless bandit country inhabited by pioneers, fur trappers and others trying to make a living within a wild and rugged world. Isabelle had a yearning to visit the valley of Estes Park, a place of extreme beauty surrounded by magnificent peaks. She travelled by horse with different people she had met, eventually deciding to stay on a ranch owned by Griffith Evans. During her stay she learnt how to drive cattle, sometimes spending as much as ten hours in the saddle, along with carrying-out many other farm chores on the ranch.

It was during her stay that she met Jim Nugent otherwise known as 'Rocky Mountain Jim'. He was a notorious gambling, drinking man of disrepute who had only one eye and a history of run-ins with the law. On seeing Longs Peak, a 4,346 metre high mountain which towered above the Estes Park valley, Isabelle developed an urge to climb it. Jim announced he would be more than pleased to be her guide. So, the two of them along with two younger men, completed the challenging climb to the mountain's summit. As time went on, a fondness developed between Isabella

Isabella's home in the Rock*y Mountains. Image courtesy of the University of Oklahoma Press*

and Jim. Alone, she then decided to explore other parts of the southern Rocky Mountains. She rode in all weathers, including deep snow, and always carried a gun. On her return to Estes Park, there was a proposal of marriage from Jim, which Isabella declined. She later wrote of Jim: 'A man any woman might love but no sane woman would marry.'

She then left the Rockies, made her way to the east coast and boarded a ship back to Britain. On her return home, Isabella set about writing another book and gave numerous talks about her travels. This, in turn, provided the necessary funds for future trips.

It didn't take long for Isabella to feel the need to travel again. Her health had deteriorated, with her familiar bad back and with feelings of depression. So, in 1878 she set sail for Japan. She arrived in a country which was steadily evolving into a more modern society. The authorities gave Isabella permission to visit the less developed and more remote far north of the country. So, it was astride a horse and with her Japanese guide named Ito, she began her journey through Japan. She spent considerable time with the Ainu people on Hokkaido, the most northerly island. She was fascinated by their way of life and the environment they lived in and made a detailed study of these inhabitants which few outsiders knew about. After Japan, Isabella visited Malaya where she enjoyed the abundance and variety of wildlife. She explored the country by boat and riding high upon elephants.

Her life changes

Whilst on her travels, Isabella would constantly write detailed and descriptive letters, the majority of which, would be sent to her sister Henrietta back on the Island of Mull in Scotland. She was her trusted confidante. These letters would then form a basis for future books. On Isabella's return to Britain, she stayed at the family home on Mull. It was there that Henrietta was diagnosed as having typhoid. The family doctor, John Bishop, and Isabella, nursed Henrietta but unfortunately her sister died. In 1881, Is-

A boat on the Min River.

abella and John were married. However, both became plagued by ill health during which, any question of further travels was out of the question. In 1886, John Bishop died, after which, Isabella was distraught, the second person close to her to die in just a few years. Her grief was accompanied with yet more ill health.

As before, she decided to travel, this time to Kashmir and Tibet. Her immediate aim was to set up a mission hospital in Srinagar in John Bishop's name. She then travelled northwards into Tibet crossing mountain passes over 5,000 metres in height, experiencing all manner of conditions which included blizzards and rugged terrain. Her party consisted of mules and their drivers, an interpreter and one Afghan soldier. On one occasion, Isabella fell from her horse and broke two of her ribs while crossing a flooded river. During the expedition, Isabella spoke of the joy travelling brought her: 'This is purely a wandering life. We never know in the morning where we shall be at night, but if a place looks nice and there is water we decide to camp there. I like it.'

Isabella's Asian adventure continued as she travelled by mule with a British military led group from Baghdad to Tehran. They journeyed through the desert during wintertime, where it was very cold and snowy and many in the party suffered frostbite. Isabella then formed her own caravan and travelled through Kurdistan. After which, it was time to return to Britain again.

Fording the Karun River from Journeys in Persia and Kurdistan

Later years

In 1894, at the age of 63, she set off for a three year trip travelling between Japan, Korea and China. It was during this journey, Isabella practised her newly acquired photographic skills. In Korea, she journeyed for five weeks in a sampan along the River Han. Then, it was up into the mountains by pony. She got caught-up in the Sino-Japanese War and witnessed the devastation that the conflict had caused in Korea. In 1896 she travelled along the Yangtze River by sampan and then overland to Sichuan where she was set upon by angry mobs calling her a 'foreign devil'. She became trapped in a house and the assailants managed to set fire to it. At the last minute, she was rescued by soldiers. On a different occasion, she was stoned and was knocked unconscious. She then travelled through the mountains of Tibet before returning to Britain.

In 1901 and in her seventies, Isabella travelled to Morocco where she rode over 1,600 kilometres with the Berbers across the desert and in the Atlas Mountains. She used a ladder to mount her large black stallion which was a gift from the Sultan.

Although she had led a life of dangerous travel and had suffered frostbite, cholera, broken bones, malaria, volcanic burns, physical attack and near drownings, she died peacefully in Edinburgh only a few months after her return in 1904. The end of, what had been, a most fascinating and varied life, crammed full of adventure.

Edward Payne Weston

Who was he?

Edward Payson Weston was an American who was famous for his nineteenth century long distance walking. During his lifetime he completed a number of walking achievements at the height of the now forgotten activity of 'pedestrianism'. In many ways, he was ahead of his time, advocating the importance of maintaining a healthy lifestyle and a need to look after our bodies. His walking feats were legendary at the time, which he continued setting, well into his later life. He justly deserves the accolade, given to him at the height of his fame, as the 'world's greatest walker.'

Early Life

Edward was born in Providence, Rhode Island, in 1839 into a middle-class family. He went to school in Boston. His father was a teacher, merchant and publisher and his mother was a writer of both poetry and novels. As he entered his teenage years he experimented with a range of jobs whilst deciding his future. He worked on a steamship, sold newspapers on the railroad, was a trainee merchant's clark, a jeweller's apprentice and he published short books about his father's trips to the Californian Gold Rush and to the Azores, as well as a novel his mother had written. He also spent time travelling around America with a group of popular singers and, at one point, ran off to join a circus in Canada where he learnt how to play the drums. While travelling with the circus, he was struck by lightening in a cart he happened to be travelling in! Unfortunately, he also became seriously ill after catching tuberculosis. His family arranged for a sports coach to ween him back to health by changing his diet and encouraging Edward to take regular daily walks. His new regime worked and he became as fit and well as he had ever been.

Edward Payne Weston.

His first walking feats

Possibly due to his colourful experiences during his earlier years, Edward had developed an interest in schemes which had the potential to make money. He became a very confident, self-promoting character, who gambled, wore flamboyant clothes and enjoyed being the centre of attention. He had become quite the showman!

During the presidential election of 1860, Edward was convinced Abraham Lincoln would lose. He was so sure, he declared to his friend, that if Lincoln won, as a forfeit, Edward would walk the almost 500 miles from Boston to Washington DC in just ten days! He said he would arrive just in time for the president's inauguration, which he would then attend. The two friends made the bet and, Edward lost! So, on 22 February 1861, Edward began his walk amidst cheering crowds and was followed by two men in a carriage to bear witness he walked the distance. During the journey, he faced heavy rain, slippery roads, high wind and deep snow conditions. He fell badly on several occasions and was chased by dogs. Passing through towns he was greeted by cheering crowds, by ladies giving him kisses and on one occasion, he had a brass band playing heartily. He ate light meals along the way and only slept for short periods wherever he could find convenient shelter.

He eventually reached the capitol on 4 March in the afternoon. Although he wasn't in time to witness the Inauguration, he wasn't too late to attend the Inaugural Ball! Therefore, Edward went along to the celebrations, during which President Lincoln personally congratulated him on his impressive walk. Edward obtained a great deal of newspaper publicity for his effort and consequently made a name for himself as being quite a walker. During the American Civil War, between 1861-65, it is believed that Edward put his obvious walking skills to good use by delivering mail to Union troops cut off behind enemy lines. On one occasion, he was arrested as a Confederate spy until he was able to convince his captors of his innocence. Around the same time, Edward married Maria Fox and within a few years, three children had been born.

Pedestrianism

Just after the Civil War in the United States, long distance walking competitions became extremely popular. Walking challenges were being made covering long distances and taking many days to complete. Such events took place, either by walking from one location to another or, as an alternative, they might take place in large arenas at one venue. The latter would allow for huge crowds to gather, sometimes in their thousands. Wagers on the outcome would be made as the competitors walked round and round a track. Money could be made by the spectators and substantial amounts could be won by competitors. Spurred on by his previous walking successes, Edward decided this money-making activity was for him. Therefore, in 1867, at the age of 28, he became a professional pedestrian. Besides being an opportunity to get rich, Edward actually enjoyed walking and was quite good at it!

In 1867, Edward took-up a challenge to walk from Portland, Maine to Chicago, Illinois, a distance of 1,200 miles. Although being physically attacked and receiving death threats from those who had bet against him winning, he covered the distance in 26 days and earned $10,000! Along the way, Edward had taken the opportunity to give lectures to some of the by-standers about the benefits of walking and the importance of leading a healthy lifestyle. He had become a great proponent of healthy living and supporter of the temperance movement.

Edward had therefore found fame in an activity which had become extremely popular in both the United States and in Europe. He didn't always win walking challenges but made enough money to live-on for himself and his family from both the prize money and personal wagers. One of Edward's successful long distance challenges was in 1869 when he walked 1,058 miles in snowy conditions in New England in 30 days. Also, in 1871, during a 200 miles walk around St Louis (part of which had to be walked backwards) he completed it in just 41 hours. Edward became the first person to walk 400 miles in five days and 500 miles in six. Although during many events Edward would become exhausted and be very close to collapse, after just a short rest, some refreshment or indeed a short sleep, he was ready to carry-on. He had become well known for his remarkable recoveries!

With his growing success and fame, he travelled to Europe in 1876, where he stayed for three years. It wasn't long before he was challenging the British pedestrian, William Perkins, to a 24 hour indoor walking duel. The walkers started off on a cold January day with the crowds all gathered and encouraging their favoured pedestrian. Late at night, the venue was emptied apart from the officials and competitors. And, there they continued walking, all through the night until 5pm when the crowds were allowed back in again. The Britain gave up after covering 65 miles in fourteen hours but Edward walked 109 miles in 24 hours!

William's boots were found to be full of blood and he was totally exhausted whereas, the American appeared to be unscathed. Edward had other successes as well as some failures during his visit across the Atlantic. In 1879, Edward managed to walk 550 miles in 142 hours, so winning the prestigious 'Pedestrian Astley Belt'! He also agreed to take part in a 5,000 mile walk around Britain to support the British Temperance Society where, as well as walking, he would give lectures in support of leading a non-alcoholic life. During some of these walking competitions in Britain, he allowed medics from the Royal Society to examine him, to which the experts declared: 'his feat is the greatest recorded labour that any human being has ever undertaken without injury.'

Weston verses O'Leary in 1877 at the Agricultural Hall in London.

An example of a failure to win a challenge was back in the United States during a 500 mile trek from Bangor, Maine to St Paul, New York and then return. It took place during winter condition which Edward found too difficult to continue walking and lost out on the $25,000 prize money. Other occasions where he failed to win were meetings with the notorious Daniel O'Leary from Chicago who managed to out-walk Edward on three different occasions. Edward continued to take part in such challenges, both winning and losing. He earned prize money, lost prize money, made personal wagers, some of which he won. However, as he got older, the inevitable happened: younger pedestrians were taking his limelight.

Later years

In later life he decided to retire from walking competitions, spending most of his time on his farm in New York State where he enjoyed taking his daily recreational walks. However, when tempted, he would temporarily come out of retirement. Reasons for such changes of mind, would be when he had run out of money or because he just missed the spectacle of a 'pedestrian's' life. However, the walking challenges he completed during his senior years, were phenomenally impressive for a man of his age.

In 1907, at the age of 68, Edward attempted to better his 1867 time for walking the 1,200 miles from Portland to Chicago. This, he succeeded in doing, cutting his time of forty years standing by over 24 hours! Then, at the age of 70, Edward decided he wanted to walk across America from coast to coast, some 4,300 miles. He planned to do it in just one hundred days.

On 16 March, 1909, he left New York and headed west planning to walk on roads and railroad tracks. Along the way, many fans urged him on. During the second half of his trek, Edward met a great number of challenges which included walking in deep snow, through torrential rain, floods, desert heat and amongst plagues of mosquitoes. He also managed to get lost on one occasion and had a number of falls. And, while crossing the Rocky

Mountains, the winds were so strong that he was forced to crawl on his hands and knees! Despite all of this, he eventually reached San Francisco in 104 days.

Unhappy with his attempt at crossing the entire country four days longer than he planned, the following year, Edward tried again. This time he walked from Santa Monica in California to

Weston in 1910 during his 3,100 mile walk across America.
Photograph courtesy of John Weiss.

New York, aiming to complete the journey in just 90 days. Edward believed that if, as a young man, he had once walked 125 miles in 24 hours, as a senior citizen, he should be capable of walking the required average of 40 miles each day. With much delight, he managed to walk from the Pacific to the Atlantic in only 76 days! A reporter from the *New Hampshire Daily Herald* spoke of the scene at the end of his walk:

Half a million people crammed New York's greatest thorough-fare today to see one white-haired man march through the cheering lines.

Edward's last great walk was in 1913, at the age of 75, when he walked 1,546 miles from New York to Minneapolis in just 51 days.

Whenever possible, Edward continued to lecture about the need for his fellow Americans to eat well and lead a healthy lifestyle, which ought to include the taking of regular exercise. He continued to decry both smoking and the drinking of alcohol. He also warned about the increasing use of automobiles in society, warning that it would result in people becoming too lazy! Edward's enthusiasm for walking can be summed-up in his own words:

Anyone can walk. It's free, like the sun by day and stars by night. All we have to do is get on our legs, and the roads will take us everywhere.

In 1927, Edward was accidentally hit by a New York taxi cab and sadly, he never walked again. Two years later in 1929, he died in his sleep at the age of 90.

Lucy Walker

Who was she?

Lucy Walker was a British woman, credited as being one of the world's greatest female mountaineers during the late 1800s. For around twenty years, she was at the forefront of female alpinism and succeeded in completing many major ascents. Lucy developed a great passion for the mountains. She was greatly impressed with their beauty, their grandeur and for the excitement and danger they brought. Lucy was an extremely good natural climber, possessing great strength and endurance. Somebody once commented that it was Lucy's 'unflinching will-power' that made her reach the summits of mountains.

Her Early Life

Lucy was born in 1836 in Canada but brought up in Liverpool by her wealthy and well established business family. She has been described as being the perfect Victorian young lady: an expert in needlecraft, widely read and proficient in a number of languages. She wasn't at all athletic during her younger years, taking part in few recreations apart from croquet. Lucy took an active role in the social life of Liverpool and was a good hostess.

It had become a family tradition, that each summer, they would all travel to the Alps. Both her father, Frank, and her younger brother, Horace, were keen climbers. They were both early members of the British Alpine Club. The family would base themselves in a variety of locations where the men would be able to walk and climb. Frank and Horace, had both become well known throughout this pioneering period of exploring in the Alps and all the major peaks were being ascended for the very first time. Victorian etiquette dictated that Lucy wouldn't have been expected to enjoy the same freedoms as her male relatives, so she kept to the valleys during alpine visits.

Lucy's climbing begins

However, a doctor recommended Lucy begin walking as a cure for rheumatism. Therefore, rather than wait around in the valleys, Lucy started to walk as much as she could during their visits to the Alps. In 1858 she scaled both the Théodule and Monte Moro passes. The following year, wanting to build upon these experiences, Lucy expressed a desire to climb Altels, a 3,629 metre peak in Switzerland. Her father, being somewhat of a visionary for the times, supported the idea. Frank suggested that Melchoir Anderegg would be the best Swiss guide to accompany them all up her first Alpine peak. The climb was a success and so began Lucy's mountaineering career and her first of many ascents with Melchoir, the only guide she ever climbed with.

Over the next few years, Lucy's climbing progressed as she completed a number of significant routes including the Monta Rosa (4,634 metres), Mont Blanc (4,808 metres) and the Eiger (3,970 metres). On her ascent of the Eiger, the party began their climb at 1am and returned at 3pm, a fourteen hour excursion. The climb hadn't been the easiest of ascents with a number of features threatening to defeat them. These included poor visibility, difficult route finding and icy conditions. Lucy was the first woman to climb the mountain. On the summit, the successful group celebrated their success by drinking champagne, eating sponge cake and participating in some very loud yodelling! That same year Lucy was part of the first ever ascent of the unclimbed Balmhorn at 3,698 metres.

Following these triumphs, Lucy went on to climb the Jungfrau,

Weisshorn, Dom, Mönch, Jungfraujoch and the Aiguille Verte. During Victorian times, just as today, these were not the most straightforward of summits to ascend. Her list of successes was increasing in length and Lucy was gaining a reputation for her climbing prowess.

Victorian attitudes

Considerable malice was often directed towards Lucy and any other females venturing to great heights. It was widely believed that a 'woman's place' was in the home supporting the male dominated society of the time. Mountain activities within society, were generally considered to be foolhardy and definitely not for

Lucy seated bottom right with her father, Frank. Melchoir Anderegg is standing at the back in the centre

a lady! Lucy would never be expected to be alone with unrelated males during these excursions, such as with her guide, Melchoir Andregg. Therefore, her climbing parties always included a family member. A further handicap for her was that she, for reasons of modesty, had to endure climbing in her voluminous, ankle length, white printed dress!

Lucy finds fame

In 1871, Lucy decided she wanted to climb the Matterhorn. Her decision had been spurred on by Melchoir's news that Meta Brevoort, an American mountaineer, was planning to become the first female to make the ascent. Although three days earlier, Lucy had made the first female ascent of the Weisshorn, she prepared herself for the climb. So, in a climbing party which included her father and Melchoir, Lucy made an attempt on the mountain from the Swiss side. Due to the number of deaths upon the mountain since being first climbed six years earlier, there was immense interest in her bid to climb the Matterhorn. On 21 August 1871, Lucy Walker stood on the summit and into the the history books, becoming the first woman to climb the iconic peak.

Lucy received both condemnation as well as some acclaim for her efforts. Not long after her climb, *Punch* magazine published a poem in her honour, the final verse being:

> *No glacier can baffle, no precipice balk her,*
> *No peak rise above her, however sublime,*
> *Give three times three cheers for intrepid Miss Walker,*
> *I say, my boys, doesn't she know how to climb!*

Lucy had suddenly become a renowned personality and in the newspaper world, an overnight success! After climbing the Matterhorn, many throughout the Alps wanted to meet this new celebrity.

She continued to journey to the mountains each summer. Over the following years her most notable successes included the Jungfrau, Täschhorn, Weisshorn, Allalinhorn and Alphubelhorn.

Lucy approached all of her climbs with enthusiasm and energy. Evidently, as she travelled around the Alps and on the climbs themselves, Lucy was a good companion to be with. She displayed a great kindness and regard for others around her, as well as possessing a good sense of humour. Whenever she could, throughout her climbing life, she always went out of her way to encourage other women and men to climb.

'Club Room of Zermatt, 1864' by James Mahoney. Lucy is the only female in the picture, standing in the doorway.
Photograph courtesy of the Matterhorn Museum, Zermatt.

Later years

In 1879, Lucy was advised by her doctor to give up her mountaineering. So, in later life during her visits to the Alps, she would walk but not climb. She would also meet with friends, including Melchoir Andregg. Lucy was once asked why she had never married, her simple reply was: 'I love mountains and Melchoir, and Melchoir already has a wife!'

Lucy had been an extremely capable mountaineer, with so many successful ascents to her name. However, she was never allowed to join the 'male only' Alpine Club in London. The decision

The Matterhorn (around the time of her ascent).
Photograph courtesy of the Matterhorn Museum, Zermatt.

of this very Victorian institution, baffled some, including Edward Whymper, who had been on the very first ascent of the Matterhorn in 1865. He once commented: '…no candidate for election in the Alpine Club… ever submitted a list of qualifications at all approaching the list of Miss Walker.'

However, Lucy did become a member of the Ladies' Alpine Club, formed in 1909. In 1913, she became its president and remained an active supporter for several years. Some have questioned why Lucy never published her memoirs. It has been suggested that by doing so would have been against her Victorian principles in remaining modest about her success. Also, she possibly didn't want to divert attention from the celebrated climbs of both her father and brother.

Lucy's climbing career had spanned some 21 years, with a total of ninety or so different summits to her credit, many of which being first ascents by a woman. It was, an extraordinary career! Lucy died in Liverpool in 1916 at the age of 81.

Thomas Stevens

Who was he?

Thomas Stevens was a prolific, daring and resourceful adventurer, most famed for being the first person to journey around the world on a penny-farthing bicycle. He also visited a number of locations around the globe, investigating different peoples and using a variety of transportation. His descriptive accounts of his many travels through his articles and books, provide a vivid historical picture of life in the places he visited.

On his penny-farthing, waving his hat.

Early Life

Thomas was born in 1854 in Berkhamstead near London, to parents who ran a grocery shop. As a child he excelled at sports, had a reputation for being a daredevil and dreamt of travelling afar, especially to America. In 1868 his father went to Missouri to clear land for a farm; Thomas was left behind in charge of both the family and the business. However, when his mother became ill, his father returned. At the age of seventeen, Thomas went to the United States, later to be joined by the rest of his family. After helping to set-up their homestead, Thomas set off on his own towards the west coast. For the next few years he held a variety of jobs throughout the American West. However, being restless by nature and needing to quench his thirst for adventure, he came up with an idea: he would cycle around the world! So, Thomas went to San Francisco where he bought a 50-inch 'Standard' bicycle, otherwise known as a 'penny-farthing'. Having never ridden a bike before, he then spent time teaching himself how to ride his new machine.

Around the world on a penny-farthing

In the April of 1884, Thomas left San Francisco at the start of his great adventure. He carried very little for his journey apart from a few clothes and a raincoat (which doubled-up as a tent) a small tool-kit and a pocket revolver. All of these items he carried in his handle-bar bag. He headed towards the Sierra Nevada mountains where, on meeting the snow, he followed railway lines. Snow-sheds had been built so trains could continue passing through the mountains during the months of winter. Going through the snow-sheds was fine, but if ever a train came along, Thomas and his bike would need to rush to the side so as not to be crushed!

Then, came the heat of the Nevada Desert, after which came the Rocky Mountains. Over much of this challenging terrain, he was often forced to push his bike. The roads, as such, were often unsuitable for riding due to the holes, mud, sand, loose rocks, snow and ice upon them. At night, he would sleep wherever he could: in hotel rooms, in people's homes, on floors or out under the stars. Thomas encountered a few wild animals during this part of the journey which included being attacked by a mountain lion as he rode through Nevada. Fortunately, he managed to frighten it off by using his gun. And, in Nebraska a rattlesnake bit his leg, but thankfully, only into the gaiters he wore.

Whenever he reached towns along the way he was often greeted with intrigue. He would then receive requests for a demonstration of his cycling skills. Onlookers were amazed to witness this new form of transportation being performed before their very eyes! In some larger settlements he would be greeted by members of 'wheelmen clubs', the cycling groups which were springing up all over the United States at that time. Thomas took to wearing a military hard hat in order to protect his head during the many occasions he took a tumble. As he made his way further east, the roads gradually improved.

By July, Thomas had reached Chicago where he rested for a while before carrying on. Eventually, he reached Boston on the east coast after travelling over 5,900 kilometres, which had taken him a total of 103 days to complete. For around one third of that journey, Thomas had to push his bicycle due to the poor condition of the roads. This was the first time that anybody had cycled from the Pacific to the Atlantic coast in the United States, an impressive transcontinental crossing. Thomas spent the winter in New York writing about his journey for the popular magazine called *Outing*. In the spring, the magazine made him a special correspondent and agreed to sponsor him for the remainder of his cycle ride around the globe.

He travelled to Liverpool by steamer to begin his European leg. In May 1885, he left Liverpool, to the cheers of around 500 on-lookers and was escorted on his way by a group of local cyclists. He visited Berkhamsted, the place he lived in before moving to America, as he made his way to the south coast of England. Crossing the Channel he then cycled through France, Germany, Austria, Hungary, Romania and Serbia, all of which he found enjoyable and

Thomas Stevens with gear tied to has handle-bar.

easy to navigate. While cycling through Hungary another cyclist joined him for hundreds of kilometres, with neither being able to speak each other's language!

On reaching Turkey, Thomas found travelling a little more demanding with constant demands for 'cycle-riding' demonstrations from large crowds wherever he went. Also, he was constantly being questioned by the police. On reaching Constantinople he bought some extra spokes for his penny-farthing, an extra tyre for his back wheel and had a tent made where he could use his upturned bike as a centre support. He was warned that during his journey ahead, he might well come across bandits. This information made Thomas decide to swop his gun for a slightly more powerful model. He then continued eastwards. As forewarned, near Mount Ararat, two men tried to rob him… However, they soon ran away when Thomas produced his new fire-arm. He rode through Kurdistan, Iraq and into Iran. Rather than battle through the snow, he spent the winter in Teheran as the guest of the Shah. After being refused permission to cycle through Siberia, Thomas had to think of an alternative route. Therefore, when spring came along, he began cycling through Afghanistan, however, he was eventually expelled from that country because he didn't have the required travel documents. With a degree of reluctance, he returned to Constantinople and boarded a ship for India.

Crossing the sub-continent, he rode westwards on the surprisingly well surfaced and bandit free, Grand Trunk Road. The road took him to Delhi and then went on to Calcutta. Even though the heat was at times unbearable, he enjoyed his cycle trip through India. Another ship took Thomas to Hong Kong where he began the most testing part of his entire journey when he crossed China. Setting-off in the south-east of the country, he had problems

Thomas on his bike with horse-riders cheering him on.

Thomas Stevens in Japan

finding his way in a land where it was difficult to obtain directions or communicate with those he met. It was unfortunate but, at that time, all foreigners were treated with great hostility and suspicion. On a number of occasions, he had to brandish his gun in threatening situations and once narrowly missed being stoned to death by a riotous mob. Five weeks after entering China, Thomas finally arrived in Shanghai. He then sailed to Japan where it took three weeks to cycle across the country. Here, he enjoyed both the friendliness of the people and their good roads, as he made his way to Yokohama. A steamer then took Thomas back to San Francisco. As he disembarked in January 1887 from his ship in San Francisco Bay, he had completed the first ever circumnavigation by bicycle. He had ridden around 21,000 kilometres!

Further adventures

Thomas published his two volume account of his global trip, *Around the World on a Bicycle* and he began a lecture tour across

America. Thomas Stevens had become a celebrity! However, it wasn't long before his innate restlessness was, once again, enveloping his thoughts. So, when the *New York World* newspaper offered him a job as a reporter to search for the missing African explorer, Henry Morton Stanley, Thomas jumped at the opportunity.

Some years previously, Stanley had found the famous explorer and missionary, David Livingstone in Africa, after he had mysteriously gone missing; now, Stanley himself had vanished, again, somewhere in Africa! He had not been heard of for around eighteen months. So, for the next six months, Thomas led a large expedition all over East Africa, searching for news of the whereabouts of Henry Morton Stanley. During his search, he travelled near to Kilimanjaro, met with the Maasai and went hunting for big game. Amazingly, Thomas did eventually meet-up with Stanley who had learnt of his search for him. After completing another book about his African encounters, the same magazine asked Thomas to turn his attentions to Russia. He was asked to investigate its people.

On reaching Moscow, Thomas bought a horse called Texas from an American travelling show. Then, over the next six weeks he rode around 1,600 kilometres on horseback to the Black Sea. He later wrote about the places he rode through and the people that he met along the way. One particular highlight of his journey was an interview with Leo Tolstoy, the Russian novelist, who he met on his estate. After completing a book about his Russian experiences, it wasn't long before Thomas was in need for more adventure.

Although having no experience of travelling by water, he bought himself a petrol-powered boat and went off to explore many of Eastern Europe's rivers. For six months he journeyed along the waterways from the Baltic Sea to the Black Sea. Again, he wrote about his journey in a series of articles. Then, for his final escapade, Thomas went off to India to investigate mysticism in that great land. His aim was to substantiate whether or not

On a horse when he rode across Russia

Hindu ascetics were capable of performing miracles. For half a year, Thomas travelled throughout India interviewing mystics and photographing any possible miracle acts they could perform. On his return to the United States, he gave lectures on his findings with a conclusion that, in his view, there were indeed miracles being performed by some Indian ascetics. After these lectures, Thomas then decided, at the age of 40 and after some 25 years of adventures, that he would bring his constant travelling to an end.

Later Life
In 1895 Thomas moved back to Britain and married Frances Vanbrugh, who was from an acting background. He eventually became the business manager of the Garrick Theatre in London.

Although his travelling days had ceased, he did occasionally write a few articles about his previous adventures. His wife died in 1917 after which, he became a First World War volunteer making artificial limbs for wounded soldiers.

He died in 1935 in London at the age of eighty. It was an end to an altogether remarkable life, of a man who had craved and embraced adventure.

John Muir

Who was he?

John Muir was a Scottish-born American naturalist, mountaineer, explorer, farmer, writer, and conservationist. He is well known for his wilderness living, his explorations and for his love of nature. His ideas on protecting natural environments, have greatly helped in the preservation of wild places. Undoubtedly, his thoughts and actions have enabled national parks to flourish worldwide for us all to enjoy. John Muir is often referred to as the 'father of the national parks'.

Early Life

John Muir was born in 1838, the third child of eight children. At the age of eleven his family emigrated from their home in Dunbar, Scotland, to a Wisconsin farm in the United States. He had a very strict religious upbringing and laboured for long hours on their farmland. It was extremely difficult to make a living from the land. As soon as they were able, all the members of the family, were expected to help-out. Although John didn't receive a great deal of schooling, he always maintained a desire to find out about everything around him, particularly regarding the natural world. He constantly pleaded with his father to be allowed to have further schooling. Eventually, his disciplinarian father relented telling John, if he wanted to have an education, he would allow him to wake before the rest of the family in order to read. To take full advantage of this concession, John began waking-up at one o'clock in the morning.

'I had gained five hours… Five hours to myself! I can hardly think of any other event of my life… as the possession of these five frosty hours.'

As well as reading, he spent the time inventing things, which he had an obvious talent for. He made a sensitive thermometer that reacted to the body heat of a person standing a few metres away. Also, he made an 'alarm bed' which tipped-out the occupant at a given hour. These inventions, along with a strong desire to get away from the hard farm-labouring regime of home, led to his entering the University of Wisconsin. Those at the university were greatly impressed with John's flair for invention, considering he had received so little in the way of a formal education. John was 22 years of age, and worked hard over the next few years during which time, he also began studying natural sciences.

He left university in 1863 and over the next few years, he worked as a mechanic in various locations including a period in Canada. During 1867, in a factory making wagon wheels, he was adjusting some machinery with a file, when the said tool slipped and the point of the file pierced his eye. John temporarily lost his

Yosemite Valley, courtesy of Library of Congress

sight, however after many months, it gradually returned. The incident had changed his life. After spending so much time in the dark, he wanted to travel and witness the wonders of the world. He was especially keen to go and view the natural world of trees, rivers, lakes and mountains. He decided to commit the rest of his life to the study of nature.

He left his home and went on a long walk all the way from Louisville in Kentucky to Savannah in Georgia, a distance of some 1,600 kilometres. As he trekked along, he absorbed the natural world he met all around him. He had originally planned to travel to the Amazon rainforest but after contracting malaria in Florida, he revised his trip. Instead, he boarded a ship to Cuba, then later, another one to Panama. He crossed the Isthmus of Panama, then sailed up the west coast, ending up in San Francisco. It didn't take long for John to feel disenchanted with the city, which led to the now famous exchange with a passerby: 'Could you tell me the quickest way out of town?'

'But, it depends where you want to go,' replied the man.

'To any place that is wild,' John exclaimed.

'Yosemite!' came the simple answer.

The Yosemite

So, at the age of 29, John Muir arrived in the Yosemite Valley, in the Californian Sierra Nevada Mountains. It was a place he immediately became enthralled with: its huge mountain and valley vistas; the rocks, waterfalls, and rivers of vivid colours; and, the big skies and abundance of nature wherever he looked. The beauty of the Yosemite took his breath away... For six years this was John Muir's home where he had a few of jobs including shepherding, running a saw mill and guiding people through his beloved mountains. However, for a great deal of his time he

Yosemite Valley, courtesy of Library of Congress

Yosemite Valley, courtesy of Library of Congress

simply travelled alone in the back country where he explored, wrote a journal and completed sketches.

He became captivated by what his senses absorbed all around him. Like a person possessed, he would shout with joy and howl as he ran around looking, touching and smelling Yosemite's natural wonders. At night, he often sat by his campfire reading and reflecting upon his discoveries of the flora, fauna and landscape he had seen during the day. Eventually, he built a small cabin by a creek. Being an inventor, he constructed the cabin so that a section of a nearby stream would flow through a corner of the room. Therefore, he would always be able to enjoy the sound of running water!

During these wanderings, he climbed many of the region's mountains and made first ascents of Cathedral Peak, Mount Ritter, Mount Hoffman and a new route up Mount Whitney. John had become a talented climber and sometimes found that he needed to extricate himself from very precarious situations. His ascents were all the more remarkable given that he climbed alone, was always far from any help if anything went wrong and never used ropes or crampons.

Writing about his climb up Mount Ritter, he noted:

> …I commenced to scale it, picking my holds with intense caution. After gaining a point about half-way to the top, I was suddenly brought to a dead stop, with arms outspread, clinging close to the face of the rock, unable to move hand or foot either up or down… But this terrible eclipse lasted only a moment… Then my trembling muscles became firm again…

All seasons throughout the year held their individual delights and temptations to go out and explore. Here he is again reflecting on a day ascending a snow gulley:

> One fine Yosemite morning after heavy snowfall, being eager to see as many avalanches as possible… I set out early to climb… Most of the way I sank waist deep… where the snow was strained [I] started an avalanche… I threw myself on my back and spread my arms to try to keep from sinking… though I was tossed here and there and lurched from side to side… I [was)] without bruise or scar.

Without John realising it, many believe he was the best mountaineer in North America during the last quarter of the nineteenth century. It is widely accepted that his lone climbs were entirely nature led. His routes up a mountain would depend on whatever intrigues of the wild lured him. John would be constantly investigating, studying and sketching. Mountain historians have admitted that it will never be known just how many climbs he made because he didn't always record them. He just wandered around the mountains allowing whatever wonders he found along the way to guide him.

He became well known throughout the Yosemite as a respected naturalist and often guided visitors to various parts of the region. He became a fixture within the mountains and was often visited

President Roosevelt standing with John Muir.

by scientists, artists and the famous. If they were in the area, time had to spent with John Muir. By 1871, after he had written a series of articles about the Sierra Nevada in a variety of publications, he had become widely appreciated all across America.

Later Life

Eventually, John left the Yosemite Valley. He travelled to Alaska where he spent time exploring and studying unmapped areas. John was the first known person to explore the Glacier Bay area of Alaska. The more he saw glaciers at work, he was convinced the Yosemite Valley had been formed by similar forces. These were the early days in the science of 'glaciation' and his groundbreaking theory about how the Yosemite had been formed, eventually became widely accepted. Due to his studies of glaciation in Alaska, which he visited on numerous occasions, the Muir Glacier was named in his honour.

At the age of 40 in 1880, John married Louie Wanda Strentzel, where he successfully managed her family's fruit farm in California. They had two children, Wanda and Helen; John became a doting father and was very much a family man. He worked hard, steadily building up the business. For many years he concentrated on both making the fruit farm a success and raising his family. He found that after making the business successful he was able to ease off. John then concentrated more on his writing and conservation work. Spending many years on their

John Muir on a 5 cent stamp.

ranch hadn't stopped John's desire to explore the wild. From time to time, he continued to visit his beloved Yosemite, made further trips to Alaska and travelled to other wild areas in the United States.

He wrote many more articles and several books, all reflecting his passion for the natural world, especially the unique environments of mountainous and wilderness locations. His writing considered the fragility of nature and its difficulty to withstand human exploitation. In 1892, he co-founded the Sierra Club, whose aim was to protect outstanding natural areas of the United States. Through his writing and by other means, he lobbied and urged influential people nationwide to support the idea of creating national parks. He believed that certain vulnerable regions of the country should be protected because they were so unique and so precious. Without such environmental controls, these areas of natural beauty would be lost to the ravages of humankind.

'Wilderness is a necessity; and mountain parks and reservations are useful not only as fountains of timber and irrigating rivers, but as fountains of life.'

He used the example from the Yosemite, where, if not curtailed, sheep and cattle would eventually destroy the natural habitats of the valley. In 1903, John went even further, by taking President Theodore Roosevelt camping in the Yosemite for three days. Whilst there, he explained to the president, why such extraordinary areas of the nation were in need of protection. No doubt John's influence, helped shape the United States' conservation policy. Eventually, after relentless lobbying, the Yosemite, Sequoia, Mount Rainier and Grand Canyon regions, were granted national park status.

John continued to work for the interests of conservation for the remainder of his life. He also continued studying and discovering the delights of nature. In 1903-4, he went on a twelve month long journey around the world looking at various special natural locations in Europe, South America, Africa, India, China, Japan and Australasia. Throughout his later life he had a number of awards and accolades bestowed upon him for his work as a naturalist and conservationist. In total, he had written over 300 articles and twelve books about a whole number of related topics.

John Muir died in 1914 in Los Angeles, at the age of 76. However, his thoughts regarding the environment lives on: the very name 'John Muir' is now synonymous with wilderness travel, nature and conservation. During his lifetime he had travelled a long way from his childhood in Scotland, to becoming one of the most important conservation thinkers in the earliest days of environmentalism.

Most importantly, John Muir's philosophy regarding conservation and caring for our wild locations, lives on to this day. The relevance and importance of protecting our environment has been embraced worldwide. An extraordinary legacy for a wholly extraordinary man!

Matthias Zurbriggen

Who was he?

Matthias Zurbriggen was one of the greatest mountaineers and guides at the turn of the last century. During the years of early mountain exploration he became a highly sought-after guide and travelled to many mountainous areas all around the world. As well as being an accomplished mountain guide, he also possessed many other skills and could speak a number of different languages. He was an immensely strong and talented climber with a natural instinct for ascending previously unclimbed mountains.

Early Life

Matthias was born in 1856 in Saas-Fee in Switzerland. As a two-year-old toddler, Matthias crossed the high Monte Moro Pass with his large family. Travelling from Switzerland into Italy, the family then settled in the village of Macugnaga at the base of the Monte

Rosa. His father managed to find work in the local gold mines along with many other migrants to the area.

So, Matthias grew-up in an awe-inspiring area of the Alps, surrounded by many iconic and beautiful mountains. His world was dominated by the Monta Rosa, the second highest mountain in the entire Alps. Unfortunately, his father was killed by a stone-fall within the mine when Matthias was just eight-years-old. Therefore, in order to help with family income, Matthias was required to work at a very early age.

Like many young mountain children throughout the Alps, he became a goat herder, looking after the creatures on the high pastures above his village. However, at the age of thirteen, feeling restless and with a desire to ease the financial burden of his family, Matthias left his home. He decided to travel, spending many years working in a range of jobs in Switzerland, France, Italy, Tunisia and Algeria. His jobs included, stableman, silver and copper miner, carpenter, cart driver and stone mason. He helped in the construction of rail tunnels, completed his military service and travelled as a hunting guide with a Swiss gentleman across North Africa.

These were all tremendous experiences in which Matthias learned a number of trades and picked-up several languages. After eleven years away, he returned to Macugnaga where he wanted to visit his family before travelling to Chile where he was aiming to find work. However, his mother persuaded him to stay in the village where he decided to open a small shop. With his many acquired skills, he also became involved in the construction of the Marinelli Hut on the Monte Rosa.

It was during this time that Matthias began climbing the local peaks. With a passion for the mountains and possessing obvious climbing skills, before long, Matthias had added an additional job to his list: that of mountain guide. He gained experience as he took his clients up many of the nearby mountains including Lyskamm, Dente Blanche, Breithorn, the Matterhorn and Monte Rosa. Matthias gained a reputation as being a skilled, safe, powerful and resourceful guide.

Journey to the Himalaya

One client Matthias climbed with, and obviously impressed, was Sir Martin Conway from Britain. He once said of Matthias:

> He desired to acquire every sort of knowledge and every sort of skill... a competent blacksmith, a good carpenter... and a most accomplished craftsman with axe and rope on the mountainside.

Therefore, in 1892 he was hired by Sir Martin to take part in one of the earliest expeditions to the Karakoram Mountains in the Himalayas. Matthias was an ideal choice for such a trip, not only for his elite guiding abilities, but for all those extra skills he possessed. Having a multi-talented member in a team could be very useful during an expedition where they would be travelling to remote places. It was essential to be self-reliant and independent. Just getting to these mountains involved a host of challenges including very long sea and overland journeys.

This was an age of pioneering where rudimentary equipment was used to survey the unknown glaciers, passes and peaks of these largely unexplored mountains. The year-long expedition was a great success with a number of new maps being drawn of the Baltoro Glacier region. A number of summits over 5,000 meters were climbed which included first ascents of both Crystal Peak (5,913 metres) and Pioneer Peak (6,890 metres), the latter being a world altitude record at the time. Illustrating the seriousness of their ascent of Pioneer Peak is found in Matthias' autobiography when he wrote:

> ...the cold began to affect Sir Martin Conway's feet... I took off his boots and vigorously rubbed his toes, till I knew the danger of frost-bite was obviated. This would, indeed, have been a melancholy contingency, for there were no doctors within 1,200 miles.

Their party, on reaching the summit of Pioneer Peak, just soaked up the extensive view of numerous distant mountains in all directions. They drank cognac, ate some food and Matthias smoked a cigar before he led them down the highest mountain to that date which had been ascended anywhere in the world! 'Who shall describe that moment of ecstasy which filled my heart with joy, after over three months' toil,' wrote Matthias.

On returning to guiding in the Alps, he was hired by Edward Whymper, who had been on the first ascent of the Matterhorn. Matthias led Whymper's party up Mont Blanc where they remained at the summit for five days. The scenes from the top were some of the best Matthias had ever witnessed, especially at dawn and dusk. Matthias didn't feel any ill-effects for being at such a high elevation for so long, unlike the other members of his party. This appears to have been a feature of this phenomenal mountain guide, in that he never suffered from any altitude sickness. Indeed, all the time he was on the Karakoram expedition, not once did he suffer.

Ready for climbing in New Zealand.

New Zealand

In 1894 Matthias was hired as a guide to journey to the Southern Alps of New Zealand with Edward FitzGerald and his group of adventurers. He led the party up a number of first ascents in the South Island including Mount Sefton, Mount Tasman, Mount Sealy, the Silberhorn and Haidinger, all of which are over 3,000 metres in height. Extreme conditions were often met during their days out climbing. The party also had their sights on Aoraki/Mount Cook, the highest peak in these New Zealand mountains. However, a party of local climbers beat Matthias' group to the top making sure foreigners didn't claim this greatest of Southern Alps prizes. However, Matthias managed to make the second ascent of the 3,764 metre high mountain some weeks later. It involved a daring solo ice climb up the east face and then along a ridge to the main summit. The Zurbriggen Ridge on Aoraki/Mount Cook is named in his honour.

Aconcagua

His next expedition was to the Andes in South America, once again as chief guide for Mr Edward FitzGerald. During the trip, numerous valley, mountain and desert areas in Argentina and Chile were successfully mapped. They also set about climbing Aconcagua (6,961 metres) the highest mountain in the Andes and in all of the Americas. On the first attempt, most of the members of the climbing group were suffering from altitude sickness. On the second attempt it was the intense cold that forced the climbers to abandon the climb. On the third, it was the combination of the cold and strong winds. On the fourth attempt, Edward FitzGerald wanted to turn back because again, he was suffering from altitude sickness. However, as they were only at around 600 metres from the summit, it was agreed that Matthias should complete the climb to the top by himself. As he stood alone at the top of Aconcagua on 14 January 1897, it was the highest a person had ever climbed before, at a new altitude record of 6,962 metres!

Matthias wrote:

…I set out for the summit of Aconcagua which I reached at 4:45 pm… Having neither pencil nor paper, I cut the date of my ascent on the handle of Mr FitzGerald's ice-axe which I had with me, and fixed it in the top of the cairn.

Aconcagua at the time of Matthias's ascent.

A further Andean first ascent was made during their trip, when Tupungato (6,570 metres) was climbed with Stuart Vine, another member of the expedition.

Later years

During 1899, Matthias guided Fanny Bullock Workman's expeditions into the Karakoram where further glaciers and their surrounding peaks were surveyed and mapped. Indeed, he returned to the glaciers and mountains he had first seen seven years before. He guided his party up the unclimbed peaks of Siegfried Horn, Mount Bullock Workman and Koser Gunge (6,401m). The latter climb set a world altitude record for a female climber.

In 1900, Matthias was the guide on an expedition to the Tian Shan in Central Asia with Prince Scipione Borghese from Italy. Their attempt to climb the Khan Tengri (7,010 metres) failed but they did manage to climb a number of lower peaks. Then, in 1902, he went back to the Karakoram, again with Fanny Bullock Workman, where further glaciers and mountains were explored and surveyed.

Whenever Matthias returned to the Alps, he would continue guiding clients up his local mountains. Over the years, Matthias had become well known for his guiding skills and was amongst the top of anybody's list when in the process of hiring a guide. He was a man who had a vast wealth of experience ascending mountains. Knowledge and skills had been accumulated from climbing mountains from all corners of the world; many of these

having been first ascents. He was very much at the summit of his profession. From a humble alpine goat herder, he had travelled a long, long way. In 1899, Mattias wrote at the end of his autobiography:

> There is one more great climb I want to complete. I should like to ascend Mount Everest. Every great mountain has a good way, and I am sure there is a good way up Mount Everest.

He was a visionary, who knew mountains and was always convinced he could find a way to the top.

Regrettably, his life suddenly took a decline in fortune. In 1907 he moved to Geneva where he gave up guiding. Also around this time, he left his wife and became an alcoholic, a vagrant and suffered from depression. Very sadly, Matthias was found dead in 1917 after having taken his own life.

It was a tragic ending to what had been a remarkably accomplished life. Above all, Matthias Zurbriggen will be remembered for being one of the world's most talented pioneer climbers and mountain guides.

Annie 'Londonderry' Kopchovsky

Who was she?

Annie Kopchovsky was a cyclist who covered thousands of kilometres in the early days of cycling. She became the first woman to journey around the world using a bicycle, a remarkable and unconventional achievement for a woman in the 1890s. She was also a pioneer in obtaining sponsorship and in the manipulation of the media. Her long cycle-ride helped to prove that women were equal to men during a time of female emancipation.

Early Life

Annie was born in 1870 in Latvia into a Jewish family. In 1875, her mother and father and their three children migrated to the United States. When she was eighteen she married Max Kopchovsky, a salesperson from Boston. Over the following four years the couple had three children. Annie also worked as an advertising agent for Boston newspapers, which suited her growing vivacious and persuasive personality.

Annie Londonderry Kopchovsky, photograph courtesy Peter Zheutlin

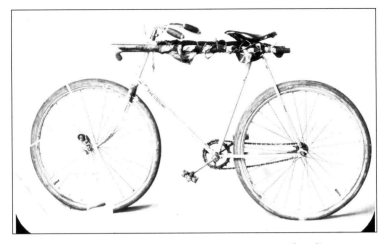

Annie's bicycle, photograph courtesy Peter Zheutlin.

Her Great Cycle Ride

During the 1890s, numerous adventures were taking place all around the world. At the same time, women's emancipation was just coming to the fore. Two wealthy men living in Boston in the USA, had an argument about whether it would be possible for a woman to complete such adventures. More specifically, it was being debated if a woman would be able to complete a circumnavigation of the globe by bicycle, just as Thomas Stevens had done some years previously. The two men agreed on a wager and decided to open the idea to any possible female takers.

On hearing about the bet, Annie decided to take up the challenge! She possibly thought it would be a perfect opportunity for her to obtain a degree of freedom, some fame and wealth – all of which, it's been suggested, she craved. Annie had been quoted as saying: 'I didn't want to spend my life at home with a baby under my apron every year.'

It was agreed that Annie should set off with no money, she wouldn't be allowed to beg but must earn a total of $5,000 en route. She would be given exactly fifteen months to complete the journey. If Annie succeeded, she would then receive a $10,000 prize! Such unusual challenges involving a wager, were very popular at the time. These bizarre undertakings were often reported with considerable enthusiasm by the press and became a much loved form of entertainment for their readers. Annie, who was employed by the newspaper industry, knew how to make the most of events in order to attract more publicity and reward.

To get her challenge underway, she managed to obtain $100 from the Londonderry Lithia Spring Water Company of New Hampshire. For this, Annie was asked to carry a placard advertising Londonderry Spring Water on her bicycle. In addition, for the duration of her journey, she was asked to alter her name to Annie 'Londonderry.' Other businesses made small adverts which Annie then placed on herself or around her bicycle.

Before departing, Annie gave herself just two days to learn how to ride a bicycle. She had never been on one before! Once she had mastered it, 23-year-old Annie was ready. For a woman to decide to leave her family commitments in the 1890s, attracted a great deal of comment. Finally, on 27 June 1894, astride her nineteen kilogram woman's Columbia bicycle and wearing a long dress, she waved goodbye to her husband and three young children. At the Boston Statehouse there were around five hundred well-wishers to wave her on her way. Many in the crowd were suffragists who had turned out to give support to Annie's attempt to equal a feat which had only been achieved by a man. She then pointed her bicycle towards New York and was on her way around the world!

Annie carried the minimum of luggage which included a change of clothing and a pearl-handled revolver. She also carried with her a great deal of determination and confidence, or as she might say in Yiddish: chutzpah. On reaching New York, she realised her clothing wasn't the most ideal for cycling her fixed wheel bike over the rough road surfaces of the day. Therefore, she decided to swop her long heavy dress for a short skirt which she wore over bloomers.

Annie then continued her journey by heading west. On parts

Annie Londonderry Kopchovsky, photograph courtesy Peter Zheutlin

of her route she was accompanied by fellow cyclists, for the activity was becoming increasingly popular at this time throughout the nation. On reaching Chicago, three months later, Annie thought she might need to amend her original plans. She was convinced her bicycle was far too heavy. In the effort of reaching the city, Annie had lost nine kilograms in weight. Therefore, she switched to a man's bicycle, which was only half the weight. In addition, she took to wearing a man's riding suit for greater comfort. Finally, Annie decided to change her direction of travel: to avoid travelling west across the continent during wintertime, she retraced her route back to New York.

NEW YORK, SUNDAY, OCTOBER 20, 180.—COPYRIGHTED BY THE PRESS PUBLISHING CO., 1895.

Bicycling Through the Arizona Desert.

Annie cycling on a railway photograph courtesy Peter Zheutlin.

In major settlements throughout her entire journey, Annie decided to give talks to interest groups or carry out a variety of tasks which would earn her funds. Part of her plan in accumulating money, was to give interviews to journalists. Being from the newspaper business, Annie knew how to create a good story; her tales were often exaggerated or entirely made-up in order to captivate both reporters and readers alike. As her journey unfolded, her fame grew which meant she was able to ask for more money for her reports and interviews.

From New York, Annie sailed to Le Harve in France whereupon, her bike was immediately impounded by customs officials. Added to this, she had discovered the money she had been carrying had been stolen. However, she managed to overcome these setbacks and cycled to Marseille in just two weeks with one short section being completed by train. The weather throughout her time in France was most inclement and included a great deal of rain and some snow, producing many muddy roads. Annie arrived at her destination despite experiencing an injured Achilles tendon and warding off some men who were trying to rob her of her few belongings. Throughout her visit to France there had been a great deal of interest in her ride. Large crowds often appeared wherever she rode and she had other cyclists join her for some sections of her journey.

She then boarded a steamship and sailed to Alexandria, Colombo, Singapore, Saigon, Hong Kong, Shanghai, Nagasaki and Yokohama. At these ports during her long sea voyage, Annie would sometimes make brief trips on her cycle, as well as obtain endorsements from the US Consul before moving on. She needed to prove she had visited each of these ports on her journey around the world in order to gain her prize.

In March 1895, Annie landed in San Francisco and she began pedalling to Los Angeles. During this section of her journey she had a male companion join her. On one occasion as they cycled along together, a runaway horse ran into them both. The two of them were injured when they fell into a barbed wire fence. Annie

MISS LONDONDERRY IN DENVER.

The Brave Little Woman is in the Best of Health, and Says She is Enjoying Her Tour Immensely.

COLORADO ROADS IDEAL FOR CYCLING.

Miss Londonderry left Boston last spring for a trip around the world on a wheel. It was a great and hazardous undertaking for a girl; but she possessed the courage, and will win her wager.

Miss Londonderry, before leaving this country, contracted with the

Londonderry Lithia Springs Water Company,

of Nashua, N. H., to use the name "Londonderry" on her journey, and to her great surprise the people of every country she visited were familiar with the name as being connected with the celebrated Londonderry Lithia Water. Thousands of people spoke of the excellency of this wonderful water.

Miss Londonderry has been highly entertained by wheelmen all through her journey. A large delegation of Denver cyclists escorted her into Denver from Colorado Springs. She will remain in the city a few days before taking up her journey eastward.

continued on through Arizona, New Mexico, Colorado and Nebraska. Again, she was often accompanied by fellow cyclists. When riding across the arid south of the United States, the heat was unbearable. The landscape she travelled through wasn't exactly conducive for smooth cycling. Selecting the most suitable route to take, became very important. Annie was often forced to cycle along the course of railroad lines; on some stretches, she resorted to travelling on the trains!

After further injury and hardship during this final stage, she finally arrived back in Boston precisely fifteen months after leaving. The cyclometer on her bicycle registered over 15,000 kilometres. As agreed during the original wager, Annie won her $10,000 prize. She had also managed to raise the required $5,000 through a range of entrepreneurial activities along the way. These included giving talks, selling pictures of herself to the public and selling the story of her journey to the press. One newspaper described her adventure as, 'the most extraordinary journey ever undertaken by a woman.'

It was indeed a daring adventure and did much to challenge the perceived position of women during these early days of emancipation.

Later Years

After her global journey, Annie and her family moved to the Bronx in New York where, she wrote for the *New York World* newspaper. She was given her own regular column under her name, with an additional byline: The New Woman. A few years later, Annie and Max had a fourth child. However, by 1900 Annie had moved away from her family and was living alone in California working as a saleslady. Sometime after that, she moved back to Max and her family and they opened a small clothing

OPPOSITE: An advertisement for one of Annie's talks appearing in the Rocky Mountain News, 12 August 1895, photograph courtesy Peter Zheutlin.

business in New York. Unfortunately, after a fire had destroyed their work premises in the 1920s, they had to start another business. Annie died in 1947 in New York, in somewhat obscurity. The story of the first woman to have cycled around the world had been lost in time.

Many years later in 2007, Peter Zheutlin came across her story. It was an interesting encounter because he just happened to be Annie's great grand nephew! Her story had largely been forgotten, nobody in his family had heard of her colourful life. As a consequence, Peter decided to write a book about his relative. It was an opportunity to remind the world about this phenomenal record breaking woman adventurer.

Mary Kingsley

Who was she?

Mary Kingsley was a woman who journeyed through West Africa during the 1890s. She travelled through its rainforests and water-ways whilst attempting to learn more about the people and the very nature of this huge but little known region. Mary took issue with the prevalent Victorian attitudes of racial superiority towards the peoples of Africa. She criticised the missionaries' interference in traditional beliefs. Mary also quietly challenged the expected roles of women within Britain at the time. In short, she was an inspirational ad-venturer and quite a radical thinker.

Early Life

Mary was born in London in 1862. Her father George was a doc-tor, who spent most of his life touring the world with various aris-tocrats. As a physician, he provided medical support for those he travelled with. He was seldom at home, often away for many months at a time. Her mother, Mary, had been a servant to George, but on becoming pregnant, he and Mary were obliged to marry. They had two children, Mary and Charles. Mary's uncle was the writer, Charles Kingsley, the author of *The Water Babies*.

Sadly, her mother had become ill when the children were small and had taken to her bed. Consequently, the household was kept very quiet with as little light as possible inside the house, to help ease her mother's condition. As was the Victorian norm in such circumstances, Mary, being a girl, took over the general running of the household and looked after her mother, while her father was away, travelling the world. Her chores included cleaning and carrying out odd jobs around their large house which was in much need of repair. Again, as was the custom of the time, as a male, Charles wasn't expected to help with any of this domestic work. He received a full education and went on to study law at Cambridge University.

By comparison, Mary's education was somewhat haphazard and was largely self taught. Her great solace were the many travel books and unusual artefacts within her father's extensive library which he had accumulated during his travels. There, she would spend a great deal of time reading and dreaming about exotic locations from around the world. It was a place where she might escape the monotony and restrictions of her life. However, whenever her father did return home, Mary would become absorbed with his many tales from his latest foreign travels.

As Mary was always fascinated by her father's trips, he eventually allowed her to research certain aspects for a book he was writing about the customs and laws of the peoples of Africa. This, she greatly enjoyed. Unfortunately, during one of his journeys, her father contracted rheumatic fever, which forced him to remain at home. Mary then had to look after two invalid parents. They both died within months of each other in 1892. So, at the age of thirty, and after carrying-out her dutiful obligations for most of her life, Mary was suddenly released of her responsibilities. If she so wished, she was free to see the world!

Mary's first visit to Africa

It was an opportunity for Mary to travel to some of the regions of the world which had fascinated her from reading and talking to her father. So, she decided to visit West Africa. For a single

woman who had lived an entirely sheltered life within her family home, it appeared to be an outrageous thing to contemplate. But, her mind was made up, even though she was warned of the many dangers including possible encounters with headhunters, crocodiles as well as the risk of catching a whole list of tropical diseases. For a lone woman to travel unchaperoned, to such a hazardous place, was unheard of! Mary believed it was an opportunity to gather ideas for her father's unfinished book about African societies. Also, as she was going to West Africa, Mary offered to collect fish and other natural specimens for the British Museum.

Her journey began in 1893, in Liverpool, where she travelled to the Canary Islands before continuing to Sierra Leone on the coast of West Africa. Then, she lived for five months with the local people in the immediate coastal region. Mary learnt about the necessary skills she would need in order to live in the rainforest. She found out how to paddle a canoe and how to use a machete when walking through the forest.

She observed all aspects of their lives, especially taking notice of their rituals, customs and witchcraft. By exchanging tobacco, cloth and gin, Mary was able to live alongside her hosts, living in their huts and eating their food. Her travels allowed Mary to study the wildlife in the immense mangrove swamps. She collected many scientific specimens including insects and fish. Mary journeyed by canoe, encountering crocodiles and on one occasion, survived a tornado.

She wrote:

> I had got caught in a tornado... The massive mighty trees were waving like a wheat field... Climbing up over a lot of rocks... where I had been half drowned in a stream... I observed right in front of my eyes... a big leopard.

On another occasion whilst paddling in her canoe, a large crocodile began clambering aboard. Giving it a huge 'clip on the snout with a paddle', she quickly paddled away. Another time, during one night, Mary managed to save a village dog from being eaten by a leopard by throwing a chair at it. The dog ran off so the large cat turned on Mary. She quickly threw a large cooking jug at the leopard which startled the creature and saved her from being mauled!

Although she was living very much as her hosts were, Mary always wore the clothes of a Victorian lady, even in the constant sweltering tropical heat and humidity of coastal Africa. She always wore a white blouse, a long black skirt, high buttoned shoes and a hat! Wearing such garments in the African heat must have been a challenge in itself. But, it was her belief that she ought not to wear clothes in Africa, she would be ashamed of wearing in Britain!

Mary developed an interest and respect for the local people she lived with. The experience she received made her denounce the actions of missionaries. She disliked the way they had destroyed local cultures and disrespected the African way of life. Equally, Mary criticised the colonial administrators who had taken over these regions. She believed they had meddled in these already well established societies and hadn't taken into account their traditional beliefs and customs. Indeed, she became quite outraged with their attitude saying:

> ...a black man is no more an underdeveloped white man than a rabbit is an underdeveloped hare.

Mary's visit to Africa's west coast had been a success. She had become fascinated by all she had experienced throughout her months of living in the region:

> I succumbed to the charm of the Coast… So I warned the Coast that I was coming back again.

Mary's second visit to Africa

In 1895, Mary returned to West Africa where she ventured further into the interior of the continent. She began her travels with the Ilgawas and M'pongwe tribal people. For almost a year she travelled along river-ways, using canoes and by walking through dense rainforest into areas very few outsiders had ever visited. On a number of occasions, her canoe capsized whilst attempting to negotiate dangerous river rapids. Journeying through the rainforest, there were always poisonous snakes and scorpions to be aware of and whilst wading through swamps, they needed to be constantly on the look-out for crocodiles. On one occasion after wading through a swamp for hours up to her chin in murky water, Mary emerged with leeches all over her body. She realised, the reason why she felt faint was due to the amount of blood the creatures had managed to extract from her!

Mary Kingsley's canoe on the Ogowé River.

As she ventured ever further, Mary came in contact with the Fang tribe, renown for their cannibalistic tendencies. Although she carried a knife and a revolver, she never had to use them. Mary was always sensitive to situations which had the potential for disaster. Due to her rapid thinking and understanding of local customs, any potential threats were usually diffused. Mary and the Fang people developed a mutual respect. Her journeys took her along the great rivers of the Remboué and Ogowé with their many rapids, mangrove swamps and dense forests.

View taken at the foot of Mount Cameroon.

Towards the end of this voyage Mary, along with members of the Fang tribe, ascended Mount Cameroon, the 4,040 metre high volcano. However, she arrived at the summit on her own because her five male companions had dropped-out further down the mountain. This was most probably the first ever ascent of the West African mountain made by a woman. Her second African visit, had also been a success, with over one hundred kilometres of waterway having been canoed and trekked. During this second journey, more information regarding the complexities of West African societies had been gathered. Respect and trust had grown between her and the indigenous groups she had met along the way. At the end of her visit, Mary had many different animal specimens to take back to the British Museum. She had managed to find one new species of fish, six subspecies, one new species of snake, and, eight new insects!

Later life

Many people came to know of Mary's extraordinary journey to Africa, so on her return, she had become somewhat of a celebrity. For the following three years, she lectured to packed audiences about her experiences, right across the country. Her travelling to Africa had created quite a stir because she had been to, what were deemed to be, dangerous locations for a single woman to venture. West Africa, at the time, was generally feared and seen to be an extremely hazardous place in which few men would dare enter! What's more, Mary had undertaken scientific research, again, which was regarded as the domain of men. Her independent journeys had discovered new species, she had contributed to geographical understanding and made anthropological conclusions. She wrote two books about her travels in West Africa: *Travels in West Africa* and *West African Studies*. She accused missionaries and colonials of trying to destroy their culture. She explained that African societies were complicated and were well suited to their environment and were not savages in need of salvation. Mary's thoughts had attempted to rock the British establishment's view of Africa.

In 1899 Mary volunteered to be a nurse during the South African Boer War. She began working in Simonstown in South Africa where she toiled for very long hours every day. She had entered a scene where men were dying in large numbers from their war injuries: from bayonet, bullet and blast wounds. However, they were also dying in their droves from typhoid. On each

of her nursing shifts, five or six patients would die from either their wounds from fighting or from the dreaded typhoid. Unfortunately, like many other nurses during the Boer War, Mary also succumbed to the disease.

She died on 3 June 1900 at the age of 37. At her request, she was buried out at sea. Her incredible life had come to an abrupt end. Mary had come to love the continent of Africa. It seems entirely appropriate that her body was given up to the waters off the coast of that great continent she had grown so very fond of.

Édouard Alfred Martel

Who was he?

Éduoard Alfred Martel was a pioneering caver who explored the underground world of numerous caves in both his native France and many other countries around the world. He was a major figure in the popularisation of the pursuit of caving and the very first truly international caver. He was not only a prolific explorer of the underworld but the creator of 'speleology', the science of caves. During his lifetime he explored over 1,500 caves worldwide and made a huge number of new subterranean discoveries.

Édouard Alfred Martel, image courtesy of the British Caving Library

Early Life

In 1859 Édouard was born into a family of lawyers in Pontoise near Paris. His first experiences into the unique world of caves was as a seven year old boy on holiday with his family. As he entered the Caves of Gargas and Eaux Chaudes in the Pyrénées, Édouard was in awe of the dark, damp but beautiful world. He was fascinated by his journey through their passages and into big chambers with their stalactites, stalagmites and other rock formations.

Developing his caving experience

Following the family tradition, Édouard went off to university to study law. Whilst there, he also developed an interest in geography and the natural sciences. During his vacations he continued visiting caves throughout France and also those further afield in Germany, Austria, Italy and Slovenia.

After completing his military service he began his life as a lawyer, practising at the Paris Bar. Although he was entering a demanding career, he still managed to find time for caving. Édouard enjoyed the challenge of underground exploration: trying to workout where the cave led to and the skills required for the journey – the ropework, use of caving ladders, winches and the challenges for travelling in subterranean water. He also began studying caves scientifically, looking at their underground water systems and geology.

Cave exploration

With an immense amount of enthusiasm, considerable daring and bravery in such dangerous environments, Édouard, continued exploring previously unknown passages and chambers. These new discoveries were significant achievements during caving's infancy when the equipment used was exceedingly basic. There was no specifically designed protective clothing and finding the way in a pitch-black world was largely carried out by candle-light. Heavy, old fashioned hemp ropes were used and descending shafts was mainly by way of cumbersome rope ladders with wooden rungs. Most explorations would involve a degree of rock-climbing, crawling, wading or swimming through a mixture of rocky, water-filled, muddy and narrow environments.

Édouard introduced the use of collapsible canvas boats and portable telephones for exploring the subterranean world. He hoped these items could improve underground travel and safety. These caving canoes were made of sail-cloth on a frame which could be taken apart and carried in a bag. Édouard recalled a trip in one of these canoes which capsized. The three people in the craft fell out into an unfamiliar underground waterway they happened to be travelling in. Their candles were immediately extinguished as they just about managed to stop themselves from being drowned. They fumbled and groped their way to safety in the total darkness. After retrieving and then lighting their candles they gathered their equipment together, after which, they continued on their exploration of the cave.

Exploration with one of Édouard's underground canoes, image courtesy of the British Caving Library.

Édouard, along with other subterranean exploring individuals he knew, would have conversations about where further trips might be made to extend certain cave systems. After their discussions, the underground journeys would then be planned and carried out. The opportunities in France for opening up fresh caves were immense. In his native country, Édouard made many new discoveries such as the Padirac Cave. In 1889 in the same cave, a major discovery was made after his party had climbed down its entrance. His group then explored this newly discovered world by using their canoe and discovered two kilometres of new passage. Later, he went on to develop the Padirac Cave into a tourist attraction. Indeed, the popularity of visiting the French caves in the Causses, Verdon and the Pyrénées regions, ever since these exploratory times, is very much due to Édouard's pioneering work.

Cave formations in the Pidirac Caves, France.

Speleology

Édouard began publishing papers and books which scientifically described cave environments. Whilst underground, he would take careful notes, photographs and measurements, and he would complete sketches and maps. They would include details about the geology, the cave formations and other information such as water features. His observations led to the birth of a new science called 'speleology'. In 1895 he founded the Société de Spéléologie

Cave formations in the Pidirac Caves, France.

which was the first ever organisation specifically devoted to the science of caves.

Through studying speleology, Édouard developed his ideas and became very vocal, expressing the importance of having a clean water supply throughout the world. This, he suggested was necessary, both above and below ground, in order to stop the

Édouard caving in Marble Arch Caves in 1895 in Northern Ireland

spread of disease. He had personal experience of this after once drinking contaminated water in a cave. Upstream from where he drank while he was caving, a dead calf lay rotting. It took him six months to fully recover. In 1895 he organised trips to Ireland and Britain where he completed significant explorations. He discovered an underground lake in the Marble Arch Caves in Northern Ireland. Using candles and magnesium flares, he discovered 300 metres of new passages.

That same year, in Yorkshire, he became the first person to descend Gaping Gill, Britain's deepest pot-hole at the time, a shaft of 98 metres. Local cavers had been making plans to go down Gaping Gill but were just pipped by Édouard. After making his daring descent using his rope ladders, he then spent two hours exploring the main chamber. During his vertical journey down Gaping Gill, he had been completely soaked by the continual water pouring down the shaft.

The following year on the island of Mallorca, Édouard discovered a huge underground lake. He also explored caves in both Belgium and Bosnia Herzegovina. In Montenegro he investigated one of the longest underground rivers in the world. Many governments would call upon Édouard's expertise and invite him to explore caves in their countries. Aline, his wife, recalls:

> …with his travelling caravan carrying rope ladders, winches, pulleys, canvas canoes, telephone, electric and magnesium light fixtures… it was the troupe of the 'Monsieur who travelled for the holes!'

Later Years

In 1899, at the age of 40, Édouard finally left his life as a lawyer in order to devote all of his time to caving. He published yet more papers and books and made more subterranean journeys. He organised further expeditions in his native France and also to Switzerland, Spain, Russia, Norway, Turkey, Portugal, Belgium, Italy and the USA. His unrelenting enthusiasm for underground exploration inspired others all around the world. By visiting many underground areas for the first time and making his pioneering investigations, he very often encouraged local cavers to make their own trips of discovery. He was a catalyst for action in many caving areas.

Towards the end of his many years involved in cave exploration, he had become the foremost expert on caving and speleology and had written a total of eighteen books and over 900 articles. For his discoveries regarding water hygiene, he was awarded the French Legion of Honour. He died in France in 1938 aged 79.

Once, while reflecting upon the exploration of caves and the

subterranean world, Édouard had said:

> No man has gone before us in these depths... nothing so strangely beautiful was ever presented to us, and... we ask each other the same question: are we dreaming?

He was undoubtedly an extraordinary pioneer of the underworld. To cavers worldwide, he came to be known quite simply as, 'The Master.'

Fanny Bullock Workman

Who was she?

Fanny Bullock Workman was an American mountaineer, cyclist, explorer, geographer, writer and a champion for women's rights. Her first adventures were as a cyclist when she completed demanding cycling trips with her husband William. Fanny then took

Fanny Bullock Workman and her husband William.

a leading role in some of the earliest climbing and exploratory expeditions in the Himalaya Mountains. Some of her accomplishments as a mountaineer in the Himalaya were quite ground breaking. Fanny refused to conform to the gender expectations of the period and was a prominent suffragist.

Her earlier life

In 1859, Fanny was born into a wealthy American family in Worcester, Massachusetts. Coming from a privileged background enabled her to attend a finishing school in New York before journeying to institutions in Paris and Dresden in order to develop her French and German language skills. On her return to the United States Fanny married William Workman, a successful physician, who was twelve years her senior. William introduced Fanny to the mountains. They spent a great deal of their summers exploring the White Mountains of New Hampshire. Fanny learnt how to climb and in doing so, developed a tremendous liking for adventure. These skills were mostly learnt in local climbing clubs which, fortunately for Fanny, offered both men and women membership. After three years of marriage, their daughter Rachel was born.

Due to the demands of his job, William was suffering from stress, so he decided to take early retirement. This life changing move happened to coincide with both Fanny and William receiving very large inheritances. Encouraged by an energetic and ambitious Fanny, they dreamt of a brand new life: they took the decision to move to Dresden in Germany. This was a perfect opportunity to escape the rigours of William's work and to begin life afresh. It was in Germany their son, Siegfried, was born. Unwilling to conform to a conventional lifestyle of wife and mother, Fanny made plans for the couple to travel and to see the world. However, such changes would have to involve leaving their daughter and son behind with governesses who would be left in charge of their daily care and upbringing.

Let the adventures begin!

Between 1892 and 1893, the couple set off to cycle through Switzerland, France and Italy. The pair decided to use the recently invented 'safety bicycles' which had the same sized wheels and a single gear. This tour was an experience they both took great delight in. Two foreigners travelling on machines, which most people had never seen before, caused significant excitement wherever they went. When their journey took them into the Alps, the temptation to climb some of the mountains along the way, was too great. Fanny became one of the first women to climb Mont Blanc.

Unfortunately, their son Siegfried, caught flu then pneumonia which led to his death. On the completion of their trip, Fanny suggested they make extended tours to locations further afield. So in 1893, the pair went off to cycle in North Africa where they travelled across Algeria, after which, in 1895 they cycled extensively around Spain. During a smaller cycling trip in 1896 they toured Switzerland, and Fanny climbed the Matterhorn and the Jungfrau. At the end of these longer trips, the couple co-wrote books and gave lectures about their adventures. They were enjoying their new life-style of freedom, exploration and challenge. All sign of William's previous work stress had vanished.

The couple then embarked on a far greater and more testing cycling challenge which lasted for more than two years. The couple cycled from the south to the north of India, some 6,400 kilometres, primarily to study its ancient architecture. They only carried the bare minimum of

Fanny with her bicycle in Algeria

supplies but stayed close to the main thoroughfares in order to replenish any provisions. It was an incredibly arduous trip where they often ran out of food and water. They were continually plagued by mosquitoes, slept in places infested with rats and were constantly subjected to punctures, sometimes as many as 40 a day! This was an altogether more demanding journey through a far more unfamiliar land.

Fanny with her climbing equipment.

The Himalaya Mountains

Fanny and William continued to explore the Indian sub-continent by venturing ever northwards into remote areas of the Himalaya. On their arrival at Srinagar in Kashmir, they suddenly saw the distant summits of extensive mountains. Cycles were left behind as they trekked 250 kilometres from Srinagar to Leh, after which, they journeyed along the Silk Road as far as the Karakoram Pass.

Over the following years they were to have seven further trips into the Himalaya. Using their personnel wealth, the Workmans were able to organise large expeditions, where huge numbers of porters were employed. Local inhabitants could easily be persuaded to join their expeditions as porters, especially when lured by the relatively large amounts of money being offered by the Workmans. The couple also hired the expertise of European mountain guides who were normally based in the Alps.

However, these trips were often fraught with problems in keeping hold of their porters. They were not always happy with the working conditions and the treatment they received during the very long journeys into inhospitable places they had never been to before. The Workmans planned each expedition meticulously with military precision. During every trip, the couple would set about surveying, mapping, photographing and then writing about the mountains, glaciers and valleys they had visited. They also spent time recording the physiological effects of altitude on those in their team.

Weeks were often spent at high altitude living in camps, while they explored glaciers, scaled mountains and carried out research. Living and journeying in the remote Himalaya Mountains during these early expeditions, meant there was always a need to be aware of inherent dangers. They needed to be self-sufficient when trekking and

Standing by her tent near the Hispar Glacier, Karakoram.

climbing in such remote and difficult terrain. Journeying through the foothills, along deep valleys, crossing raging rivers, walking over mountain moraine and across glaciers, was not without its perils. Some of the peaks they scaled had never been climbed before and many hadn't even been named.

Fanny and William very much enjoyed being in the Himalaya. Fanny wrote:

> We had breathed the atmosphere of that great mountain-world, had drunk of the swirling waters of its glaciers, and feasted our eyes on the incomparable beauty and majesty of its towering peaks...

They visited many areas in the Himalaya. In the Karakoram they were forced from the Biafo Glacier because of numerous crevasses and bad weather hindered their progress. They journeyed to the Skoro La Glacier and the unclimbed peaks surrounding it. Two of the peaks were then climbed and named: Siegfriedhorn (5,700 metres) and Mount Bullock Workman (5,930 metres). Fanny then climbed Koser Gunge at 6,400 metres, her third successive climbing altitude record for a woman. This turned out to be a challenging climb where the climbers had to camp overnight at 5,500 metres. It involved having to ascend a difficult wall in strong winds. Also, it was extremely cold; Fanny had problems holding her ice-axe because she had lost all feeling in her fingers. On reaching the summit, they stayed just long enough to establish the height of the peak using their instruments.

After these mountain challenges and before returning to Europe, they took to their cycles once again as they travelled through Sumatra, Thailand and Burma. In 1891, Fanny and William were back in Srinagar preparing for another expedition. They then explored the Chogo Lungma Glacier in the Karakoram, again using local porters and accompanied by the accomplished Swiss guide, Matthias Zurbriggen.

The following year, the Workmans returned and explored the Chogo Lungma, Hispar and Biafo Glaciers where again, they

Baltistan Himalaya, on the summit of Mount Buspar.

surveyed the glaciers and the surrounding mountains. This involved camping at very high altitudes and being subjected to numerous snow storms. Camping so high up never seemed to bother Fanny as she appeared to be immune to altitude sickness. After these long expeditions, the Workmans would return to Europe where Fanny gave lectures in English, German and French. These lectures were popular and were always received with great acclaim. At one talk in Lyon in France, a total of 1,000 people attended with 700 having to be turned away!

Returning to Kashmir in 1906, their next project was to explore the Nun Kun massif. Having had a succession of local porter problems with previous trips, they decided to take along a few Italian porters to work alongside the local ones. On this trip, Fanny achieved her greatest mountaineering achievement by climbing Pinnacle Peak at a height of 6,930 metres. It was an amazing accomplishment using the very basic equipment of the day and climbed in her usual full length skirt! Furthermore, it was a women's altitude record that remained unbroken until 1934. These Himalayan ascents were extremely challenging and Fanny developed a reputation for being a determined, strong and methodical climber.

On hearing that a fellow American, Annie Smith Peck, had surpassed Fanny's altitude record in South America, the Workmans were not pleased. Fanny and William spent a considerable amount of effort, time and money sending a team of French surveyors to the Andes to carefully check and re-measure the height of Peck's mountain! Peck's South American height was surveyed as being 6,761 metres, which confirmed that Fanny's altitude record of 6,952 metres, was upheld.

On their next Himalayan trips, the Workmans traversed the 61 kilometre long Hispar Glacier, then went over the 5,300 metres Hispar Pass and down the 60 kilometre Biafo Glacier. They were the first to survey and produce a map of the region. Their next expedition took them to the extensive Siachen Glacier in the Karakoram, where they produced a map and climbed several more

Fanny holding up a 'Votes For Women' message on the Siachen Glacier, Karakoram.

mountains. Unfortunately, one of their Italian guides, fell into a
crevasse and died. In a somewhat desperate situation, Fanny led
her group to safety by crossing the 5,700 metre Sia La Pass. It
was on this same expedition Fanny unfurled a 'Votes for Women'

newspaper while William took the picture.

After each of these expeditions, they again, produced books describing their Himalayan accomplishments. Within each document there were also details of their scientific findings and surveys. In total, in all of their adventurous life together, the Workmans co-wrote eight books along with producing a number of magazine articles.

Later in life

Fanny's work on glaciation in the Himalaya was considered to be of great value. Amongst the many institutions where she talked about this work, she became the first American woman to lecture at the Sorbonne in Paris about her discoveries. Consequently, she was awarded medals from ten different European geographical societies. She became one of the first women to speak at the Royal Geographical Society in Britain. Fanny was also honoured by a number of national mountaineering clubs including Club Alpino Italiano, Club Alpin Francais and the American Alpine Club.

After 1912, the Workmans ceased travelling to the Himalaya due to the difficult conditions before the onset of the First World War. The situation in Europe also led to their moving from Germany to the south of France. Fanny continued to support the feminist movement. She believed her life to be a role model for other females wishing to travel or take part in mountaineering adventures.

Fanny fell ill in 1917 and died in 1925 at the age of 66. William lived until 1937, dying at the age of 91. The couple had made a formidable adventurous partnership. For Fanny's part in their long list of remarkable adventures, she will be best remembered for her drive, pioneering spirit, mountaineering prowess and her tussle with conformity.

Fridtjof Nansen

Who was he?

Fridtjof Nansen was a Norwegian adventurer, explorer, scientist, diplomat, humanitarian and Nobel Peace Prize winner. He was a visionary of Arctic exploration, possessing both skills and fortitude in both his Greenland and his *Fram* expedition in the Arctic. Fridtjof's life after his adventurous feats, was equally as impressive, with certain aspects being of historical significance.

Early Life

Fridtjof was born in 1868 in Christiania (now Oslo). His father, Baldur, was a lawyer and his mother, Adelaide, was from the Norwegian aristocracy. Both parents had been married before so Fridtjof had older brothers and sisters, from previous marriages, as well as having one younger brother. He grew up in the family home situated in the Nordmarka hills, just outside Christiania. All around their home was undulating countryside with streams, lakes and forests. It was a glorious paradise for children to grow up in. During the summer there was swimming and fishing to enjoy; in the autumn older ones could hunt; and during wintertime, it was possible to ski and explore all across a snowbound landscape. As a child he spent a great deal of his time enjoying these natural delights in the wilds of Nordmarka. Fridtjof became a very good swimmer and developed his hunting skills. He also learnt how to ski when he was just two years of age and went on to become both an accomplished skier and ice-skater.

When he was older, he studied zoology at the Royal Frederick University in Christiania. Whilst at the university he joined a whale and seal hunting expedition to the Jan Mayen Islands in the Arctic Ocean. As an on-board science student he kept records of the wind, ocean currents, ice movements and the animal life they came in contact with. The entire experience in the far north was inspirational for Fridtjof where he had an opportunity to consider possible future Arctic travels. On his return after five months at sea, he was offered the post of curator of the natural history collection at Bergen Museum. For a young man of twenty, this was quite an opportunity. For the following six years, he spent most of his professional life studying the smallest of sea creatures. Moreover, Fridtjof concentrated on the workings of the central nervous system in minute marine organisms. For such detailed work, he was awarded a doctorate. However, having spent so much time labouring intensively within his laboratory, it had kept him from any of his ambitions within the wild outdoors.

The Crossing of Greenland

Determined to get back to the outdoors Fridtjof left his post in Bergen to prepare for a crossing of Greenland, a journey which had never before been achieved. Those who had previously attempted the challenge, had set-off from the west coast of Greenland and travelled eastwards before deciding to return, after meeting difficulties. However, Fridtjof's plan was to make an east to west crossing. His thinking was that once having arrived on the east coast, a party would then have little option but to travel

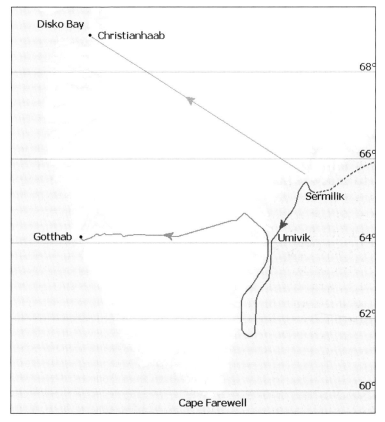

Map of the Greenland Crossing (the higher arrow the proposed route, the lower the eventual route).

westwards. This would be necessary in order to catch a ship back to Norway, as they didn't land on the eastern coast.

Fridtjof selected five companions to accompany him on his expedition, three other Norwegians and two Sami from the far north of Norway. They eventually arrived off the east coast of Greenland in a seal-hunting vessel. For weeks the ship attempted to navigate its way through the many drifts of ice so they could land. But, it was impossible! In desperation, they unloaded their equipment into two rowing boats, to try to find a way through. After many exhausting days, they unloaded their boats and then hauled their laden sledges up steep and heavily crevassed glaciers to begin their journey across the ice-cap. All the time they were hampered by bad weather. The gradient eventually eased, they then spent many days pulling their five sledges across the difficult terrain made up of both hard ice and softer snow.

Sledging across Greenland, photo courtesy of Tromsø Museum.

After reaching their highest point on the ice at 2,720 metres, their journey speeded up as they descended. There were some days when they could lash sledges together and put-up improvised sails to increase their speed. Finally, they arrived at the heavily crevassed glacier's edge on the other side of the ice-cap. It had taken 42 days to complete the first ever crossing of Greenland. The successful party then overwintered with some Inuit living on the west coast, before catching a ship out, the following spring. Returning to Norway, Nansen and his companions became national heroes.

On his return, there followed a flurry of lectures at home and abroad about their successful crossing of Greenland. In 1889, he married the popular operatic singer, Eva Sars. Like her husband, she too was an enthusiastic skier and gave great support to the idea of women competing in winter sports, just as men could.

The Fram Expedition

In 1891, Fridtjof made plans for his next expedition, this time, to the North Pole. As a scientist, he had calculated that it should be possible to arrive at the North Pole by utilising the strong ocean currents. He believed that if a ship were to become trapped in the sea-ice off the north coast of Siberia, the currents would naturally take it to the North Pole. His plan was to build a ship with a reinforced hull which would be able to withstand the pressures and just ride-up onto the ice. It was a bold idea. Work began after securing financial support from a number of quarters. The completed vessel was named the *Fram* meaning 'forward'; the naming ceremony was carried-out by Eva Nansen. After selecting a crew, enough coal and provisions were taken onboard to last twelve men for four years.

The *Fram* set sail in June 1893 and made its way along the coast as far as the New Siberian Islands in the Arctic Ocean. By September, the *Fram* had frozen fast into the sea-ice and, as predicted, it then rose up onto the ice without being crushed. While the ship drifted in the sea-ice, the crew went about a daily routine of carrying-out scientific experiments along with a range of domestic chores. However, the *Fram*'s drift was a little inconsistent in its direction, sometimes travelling northward, sometimes in other directions, and not always at the same speed. By December, they had reached 79 degrees North, by the following May, 81 degrees North. Fridtjof worked-out that if the rate of progress continued, it would take them a great deal longer than planned to reach the North Pole.

Therefore, Fridtjof decided that he and a fellow crew member, Hjalmar Johansen, would attempt to ski to the North Pole. Lashing all their provisions, two kayaks, and other equipment, to dogsledges, they left the *Fram* in early March 1895. They were entirely on their own for a push to the North Pole.

'No communication with the outside world or retreat was possible, and they would have no chance of finding the *Fram* again. They were left completely to their own devices on the path to the unknown,' said Fridtjof's granddaughter, Marit Greve, writing about the attempt.

It was agreed the *Fram* would wait for the ice to melt then make its way back to Norway. After reaching the North Pole, the pair planned to make for the nearest land. In case of the ice melting, they were also taking kayaks with them. Travelling over the ice was extremely challenging as they continually met many tall ridges of ice which were

Setting off for the North Pole from the Fram.

difficult to haul the sledges across. At other times, they were also confronted with huge areas of open-water. Therefore, progress was slow. But, with an enormous amount of physical effort, by mid-April, they had reached 86 degrees North. It was the farthest north any person had ever reached in history. Nansen calculated they would not have enough time or food to travel the entire distance to the North Pole, so reluctantly, they decided to make their way to the nearest land. Hjalmar wrote:

> Should have liked it if we could have got further. It is our consolation that we have done what we could and that we have lifted a little more of the veil which conceals this part of our planet.

Over-wintering on Franz Josef Land inside their shelter covered with snow

They then made for Franz Josef Land. The days were warming so the sea-ice was melting, therefore they found they were having to alternate between using sledges and kayaks. With diminishing food supplies, this was hard work. In early August, Hjalmar was attacked by a polar bear. He was literally pinned-down on the ice and couldn't move. He was doing his best to fight the creature and had his hands around its large neck. He calmly informed Fridtjof of his situation: 'You had better hurry, otherwise it will be too late.'

After which, his companion had found their rifle and shot the bear. Fortunately, by the middle of the same month they reached land. They realised they would need to build a small shelter if they were going to survive the encroaching winter season. Using stones, moss, driftwood and the skins of walruses, they made a stone-hut they named the den. By shooting walruses, polar bears and seals, they amassed a supply of meat, blubber and skins. With the skins, extra clothing was made and flooring for the den. And, there they stayed, inside their hovel, for the long dark and very cold winter.

Inside their shelter in Franz Josef Land. Image courtesy of Skyline Publishing

Their faces gradually darkened with grime from their basic oil lamps and they hardly ventured outside. Much of the time the pair were hunkered-down in their woollen sleeping bags while storms regularly blasted outside in the continual darkness of the Arctic winter. They lived off their meat supplies, had very little to do and just sat it out – surviving. However, they did manage to keep a journal each and, given the circumstances, their friendship remained strong. At Christmas time they marked the occasion as best they could:

> But we are celebrating in our modest way. Johansen has turned his shirt inside out… but I have also changed my underpants… I have also had a complete wash-down in a quarter of a cup of warm water using my discarded underpants as sponge and towel…

By the middle of May, the conditions were suitable to continue their journey. After being inactive for months, they found it extremely challenging to make much headway. They incurred a number of dangerous incidents. On one occasion, both kayaks had floated off so Fridtjof swam in the freezing water conditions to retrieve them. Eventually, and to their great surprise, they encountered a British expedition on another of the Franz Josef Islands.

Searching for land after their attempt at reaching the North Pole.
Photograph courtesy of the Tromsø Museum

They travelled with the expedition back to Norway. It was there they heard the news the *Fram* was safe. After the polar ice had melted enough, the vessel had managed to break-free. This entire extraordinary story of Arctic survival was greeted with huge celebration throughout Norway and beyond.

Fram crew members in front of their ship the 'Fram'

Later Life

Fridtjof gradually adjusted to life back in Christiania, which wasn't easy, given his new internationally acclaimed status. The celebration around this Norwegian expedition, along with numerous other historical grievances, had helped stoke a call for Norway's complete independence from Sweden. Addressing a large crowd in the centre of Christiania, Fridtjof said:

> Now have all ways of retreat been closed. Now remains only one path, the way forward, perhaps through difficulties and hardships, but forward for our country, to a free Norway.

Fridtjof became directly involved in behind the scenes pressure and was appointed ambassador to London in an attempt to gain international support. Finally, on achieving independence after a referendum, Fridtjof was sent to Denmark to ask their prince to become the king of the new nation, which he succeeded in doing.

After catching pneumonia, Eva died in 1907. Fridtjof resigned from his post in London and returned to Oslo to look after his family of five children. He then returned to his scientific work and became Professor of Oceanography at the University of Oslo. Another family tragedy occurred when one of his children died of meningitis – losing both his wife and a child had a huge effect on Fridtjof.

In 1919, he married again, to Sigrun Munthe, a woman he had known for many years. At the onset of World War One, he became a diplomat in Washington in the United States where he worked for the newly formed League of Nations as a humanitarian aid envoy. He was involved in the repatriation of war prisoners including Russian refugees in 1921, along with Greek and

Hauling on the sea ice.

Armenian refugees during 1922. Fridtjof was also involved in famine relief in Russia. For these significant and life-saving humanitarian acts, he was awarded the Nobel Peace Prize in 1922.

Fridtjof Nansen died in 1930. To mark the loss of this popular national and international hero who had experienced such an extraordinarily varied and awe-inspiring life, he was given a state funeral.

Annie Smith Peck

Who was she?

Annie Smith Peck was an American mountaineer who held a passion for climbing mountains in North America, South America and Europe. Some of her later climbs in South America included previously unclimbed peaks. Her climbing feats took place at a time when mountaineering was in its infancy. Her adventures are all the more impressive given that such pursuits by women were actively discouraged by society. She was also an academic, a writer, lecturer and suffragist.

MISS ANNIE S PECK

Early Life

Annie was born in 1850 in Rhode Island in the United States. At school she achieved considerable academic success, later gaining a degree in classical languages from Michigan University. For the next level in her formal learning, Annie had to try to convince people to allow her to continue. She wanted to attain a higher level of education than was the norm for women during this period '... to show that women had as much brains as men and could do things as well...' Eventually, she went on to obtain a masters degree in Greek from the University of Michigan. Next, she went off to Germany where she studied German and Music. After that, Annie became the first female student to study at the American School of Classical Studies in Athens. On her return to the USA, she taught and lectured at a number of colleges.

European encounters

Annie acquired a love for the mountains in her early thirties when she first visited the Adirondack Mountains in the north-east of the United States. This life-changing visit was during her 1882 summer vacation, after which, she tried to climb mountains whenever she could. She climbed Clouds Rest (3,027 metres) in the Yosemite with her brother and she also ascended Mount Shasta (4,322 metres) in California. Throughout the 1890s, Annie also spent many of her summer days climbing the Presidential Range in New Hampshire. She possessed a natural talent for climbing, showing an equal measure of physical strength, endurance and courage.

When Annie went off to Europe, she climbed a number of minor peaks in Greece which included Mount Hymettus and Mount Pentelicus and also Cape Misenum in Italy. Inevitably, she ventured forth on her first explorations into the Alps. In 1895, at the age of 45, she climbed the Jungfrua in Switzerland. After which, she climbed the Wellenkuppe and the Breithorn, using them as practise peaks before she climbed the more testing Matterhorn. Annie had first seen the mountain some ten years previously while on a railway journey through Europe. On viewing the peak for the first time, she was immediately impressed by its classic mountain form and vowed to return one day and climb it. Annie was amongst the first batch of women to reach the top of the Matterhorn during those early ascents of the mountain.

Annie became famous for her climbing of this classic 4,478 metres high peak. The Matterhorn was one of the most technical and demanding mountains to ascend in the Alps at that time. However, her fame wasn't so much for her very accomplished ascent, but for the clothes she wore! Annie had decided to climb in more practical and comfortable trousers rather than a long dress, which was the normal attire for women. Her outfit for climbing included knickerbockers, a tunic, sturdy boots, woollen socks, completed by a felt hat and veil. Her scandalous decision to wear trousers, could quite easily have led to her arrest! The whole affair caused considerable debate in both the American and European press, as to what was the most appropriate female clothing to use in the mountains!

Later, in 1900, her Alpine conquests included the Fünffingerspitze, Monte Cristallo and the Zugspitze. By this time Annie was enjoying a life of lecturing in various parts of the world and writing about her travels and experiences, especially those regarding mountain climbing. Although she was an academic and could deliver lectures on a range of subjects including classical studies and archeology, it was often her mountaineering talks which people were most drawn to. Her exploits amongst the peaks had given Annie considerable fame and status.

Latin American climbing records

Annie's next travels took her to South America where, once again, she explored the mountains as well as finding material for future lectures and writing. On visiting Bolivia she climbed Illampu Peak at 6,368 metres. And, in Mexico in 1897, she climbed Mount Popocatepetl at 5,426 metres along with Pico de Orizaba at 5,636 metres. The latter was the third highest mountain in North America. On climbing the peak, Annie had set a new women's altitude record. It was during this period that Annie's mountaineering aspirations attained a new aim: she wanted to ascend a major peak which previously hadn't been climbed.

> My next thought was to do a little genuine exploration, to conquer a virgin peak, to attain some height where 'no man' had previously stood.

Over time, Annie had become a staunch supporter of the growing women's movement, so her objective would indeed be a mountain that hadn't been climbed by any 'man'!

Mountaineering at such heights was no mean feat because the equipment of the period was extremely rudimentary. After all, these were pioneering times in all high mountain areas of the world. As a woman, she sometimes found it necessary to design, adapt and make her own clothing because the few items which were available, were only made for men. Although she made a certain amount of money from her lecturing and writing, Annie invariably encountered difficulties in finding financial support for her trips to any remote areas of South America. Annie hoped that by climbing a virgin peak would perhaps encourage more people to want to hear her speak when she eventually held lectures about any conquest. This would then provide much needed funds for future trips. Annie eventually climbed her virgin peak. In 1908 and on her sixth attempt, she successfully ascended the North Peak of Mount Huascarán at 6,768m in Peru. This was a huge accomplishment at the age of 58!

Initially, Annie had estimated the height of the North Peak to be much higher. Circumstances hadn't allowed her to make an

Annie's climbing party outside her tent and pictured below, Mount Huascarán in Peru at the time of climbing.

accurate measurement of the mountain's correct height. Annie believed her peak was the highest in all of South America which in turn, would give her a new worldwide women's altitude record. However, Fanny Bullock Workman, an American who had pioneered new climbs in the Himalaya, disputed her claim and decided to send a party to properly measure the mountain. After considerable effort, time and money, the North Peak of Huascarán was accurately measured through triangulation. Annie's mountain was found to be lower than the Himalayan peak her adversary had climbed. However, this revelation didn't take any of the euphoria away from her getting to the summit of a previously unclimbed

Annie Smith Peck wearing her high altitude clothes.

major mountain. In recognition of Annie's achievement, the Peruvian Government renamed the north peak Cumbre Aña Peck.

Later life

Annie continued to climb and in 1911 ascended the south-eastern summit of Mount Coropuna at 6,377 metres in Peru, which was another first ascent. Leading up to the successful climb had become a duel between Annie and a fellow American called Hiram Bingham. Both wanted to be the first to conquer this hitherto unclimbed peak. Adding fuel to the competition was the difference in their backgrounds: Annie a free-spirited, independent woman, whilst Hiram was very much of the old-school, believing that mountaineering wasn't an activity for women to be involved in. So Annie, on gaining the summit first, wouldn't have pleased her rival. On reaching the summit, and as a keen suffragist, she unfurled a banner which read 'Votes for Women'. Needless to say, this caused a sensation in many quarters all across the world!

In her later years, Annie continued to promote the ideals of the women's movement. She also wrote books relating to her South American climbing experiences as well as books about tourism and business development within that continent. Between 1929 and 1930, and aged almost 80, she spent seven months flying around South America. It was an opportunity to promote air tourism and illustrate just how safe travelling in the continent was. Afterwards, she published her book, *Flying Over South America: Twenty Thousand Miles by Air.*

Annie received a number of awards from different South American nations for her contributions to different aspects of the continent's development. Annie never married, which was a decision taken earlier in her life. Her longevity allowed her to carry-on climbing into old age. Annie climbed her last mountain, Mount Madison in New Hampshire, at the age of 82! She died in New York in 1935, aged 85. Once, when she was asked about why she enjoyed climbing mountains, Annie had replied:

> The mountains… attract me because of their grandeur, their magnificent scenery, but I climb them… not simply for the view from the summit, but because I enjoy the climb. I really love precipices and cliffs.

Upon Annie Smith Peck's gravestone are the words:

"You have brought uncommon glory to women of all time."

Dumitru Dan

Who was he?

Dumitru Dan, became the first person to walk around the world. It was a phenomenal effort of endurance which began in 1910 and was finally completed in 1923. This very long hike across many countries was an epic journey filled with both triumph and tragedy. What started off as an adventure for four friends and their dog, ended-up with only Dumitru completing the journey.

Before the walk began

Dumitru was born and brought up in the town of Buhusi in the north-east of Romania. In 1908, he went off to study at the Faculty of Geography in Paris.

Whilst there he met and became friends with three other students from his country: Paul Pârvu, Gheorghe Negreanu and Alexandru Pascu. The four

*Dumitru Dan in national costume.
Photograph permission of the Buzau
County Museum*

132

Romanian students heard about a competition which had been launched by the Touring Club de France, a French sports and tourism agency. The announcement stated: 'Whosoever can walk around the world will receive one golden Franc per kilometre'.

Although they were in the middle of their university courses, the four students decided to take-up the challenge! The Touring Club de France rules required the four friends to take some time to prepare for their global trek. They worked-out a route, learnt about the locations they would be visiting and about the conditions they would encounter. Between them, they learnt a smattering of different languages required for the trip.

They decided to wear traditional Romanian costumes and hold concerts of music and dance along the way. So, the four set about learning a repertoire of songs and dances to perform. These concerts would enable them to earn money on their journey. Also, in order to accumulate the maximum number of kilometres during long sea crossings, they decided to walk around the decks of ships using pedometers. The distances they walked would then be verified by the captain. In the many locations they visited, they would also require corroboration from the various authorities. Without proof of their visits, they would be unable to claim their prize!

Left to right, Paul Pârvu, Gheorghe Negreanu, Alexandru Pascu and Dumitru Dan. Photograph by kind permission of the Buzau County Museum

Walking around the world

In 1910 the four friends, along with their dog Harap, were ready to start walking. They had all agreed it would be a great idea to have the company of Harap on their journey. From Bucharest, under grey skies and drizzle, they began their global trek. It was

a matter of establishing a routine of walking, eating and then sleeping. Each night they planned to find any suitable accommodation available, which might be in local houses, in outbuildings or under the stars.

After many days they reached Vienna. There, they performed their first folk concert which was a great success. Next, they walked to Prague, Dresden, Berlin and Hamberg before crossing into Denmark. Next, came the cities of Christiana, Stockholm then Helsinki. On their arrival in St. Petersburg they took a rest, saw the sights and performed. It then took another twelve days to walk through the Russian countryside to Moscow. Continuing down into the mountains of the Caucasus, they took great delight in the beauty of the land-

Dumitru Dan in national costume.
Photograph permission of the Buzau
County Museum

scape they saw all around them. They were constantly checking their location and direction. During one night, as they camped out in the open in the mountains, Harap's barking alerted them to nearby wolves.

They journeyed to Tehran, and then onwards to Baghdad where they spent time just looking around the city. Next came Syria, the Lebanon and then Egypt. In such arid parts, the dry conditions along with the punishing heat, made walking very difficult. Finding enough water was a problem and they all suffered from sunburn. They were received well whenever they performed their

Dumitru Dan, by kind permission of the Buzau County Museum

Romanian folk concerts in different settlements. As planned, this allowed them to earn much needed money. Such funds were then spent in the purchase of supplies as well as any tickets required for their journeys aboard ships.

After resting in Cairo, they walked south to the Sudan and into Abyssinia, keeping close to the Red Sea. Officials in Abyssinia provided a guide to escort them through the most dangerous parts of the country. Eventually, after further debilitating conditions, more heat, rough terrain, difficulties with communicating and obtaining food, they arrived in Tanganyika. They then boarded a ship sailing to Australia.

During their sea journey, as planned, they took to walking around the deck, sometimes for as long as ten hours per day. Invariably, this rather unusual activity, caused much amusement for others onboard! When they had completed their on-board trek, the distances for that day would then be verified by the captain. Disembarking at Adelaide they made their way to Melbourne, then Sydney and eventually to Brisbane. In the cities, they were able to perform and, to their surprise, meet fellow Romanians who had emigrated to this far away land. From Brisbane they took to the sea once again, this time to the Dutch East Indies where a number of the islands were visited. From there, another ship took them to Cape Town, and they continued northwards, eventually to Italy.

Many months were then spent walking in the west of Europe, through Italy, Switzerland, France, Belgium and into Britain. And of course, along the way, whenever possible, they would perform their concerts. They arrived in the port of Glasgow, not long after the *Titanic* disaster which had taken place in 1912. The four travellers were subsequently presented with free tickets to sail to Canada. Few people were wishing to travel across the Atlantic because of a general fear of hitting an iceberg and sinking! The journey across to Quebec took ten days with further walking around the deck.

Newspaper articles of their arrival appeared in

Un giramondo

Demetrio Dann, di nazionalità rumena, sta effettuando il giro del mondo a piedi. Ha già percorso 98.300 chilometri, in 5 anni e 10 mesi, attraversando 75 Stati e consumando 408 paia di sandali.

(Fot. Campanelli - Novara)

One of many newspaper articles that followed the group's progress around the world. By kind permission of the Buzau County Museum

Dumitru Dan's passport with his many stamps and, below, endorsements of visits to different cities and towns around the world. Images with kind permission of the Buzau County Museum.

the press alerting the inhabitants that the four travelling Romanians were in North America. Consequently, their journey across Canada and the United States included giving a number of performances in different settlements. They made their way to New York and visited the Romanian community in the city where they were warmly welcomed. After which, the four made their way to Washington and were received in the White House. At the border with Mexico, they were held up because of skirmishes taking place because of the ongoing revolution. It was then a journey through the small republics as far as Panama.

137

Time to board a ship for a long 27 day crossing to Japan. They travelled from Tokyo to Kyushu, before arriving in India after a further journey by ship. They arrived in Bombay on the east coast of India. The *Times of India* had written an article about the Romanian visitors. A group of well-wishers had assembled to greet them. There was an expectation of a concert to be performed during their stay in the city. On 17 July 1913, they received an invitation from the Rajah of Bombay to stay with him while they were in the city, which they accepted. Needing to replenish their supplies, three of the group went off to purchase certain items. However, Alexandru remained behind with the Rajah with a number of other guests. A feast was produced and people gathered around listening to Alexandru's tales of the group's hike across the world. At some point, an opium pipe appeared, which was duly shared amongst those in attendance. The Romanian wanderer, having never smoked the drug before, was soon feeling very ill – sadly, he collapsed and died. On their return, his three friends were in utter shock.

Dumitru, Paul and Gheorghe were completely distraught at the loss of their friend. However, after much discussion, they made the decision to continue their journey. It took them many days of walking, to cross India and arrive in Calcutta. Then, they walked into Burma and on into China. They were met with extremely difficult walking conditions and came into contact with people who were often hostile to foreigners. While they were trekking through a steep mountain pass in the Nanling Mountains, Gheorghe fell down a steep slope and was very badly injured. In the heavy rain, he had slipped in the mud and had fallen into a ravine some eight metres deep.

The nearest town was a considerable distance away. His two companions carried him there in the hope of obtaining some medical assistance. They found help but, due to his many injuries, Gheorghe became the second victim of the journey. It came as another incredible shock. But, in that far away, unfamiliar land, the two remaining friends continued to walk. They had no choice.

Further on, during their journey through China, Dumitru and Paul were attacked and had their money stolen.

They carried-on and made their way into Siberia. The extreme temperatures and more difficult terrain made this part of their journey the most testing they had encountered to date. The Romanians bought warmer clothes, fur coats and a sleigh. Their progress was challenging in the extreme cold and winter snow. They managed to find a boat that would take them across the Sea of Okhotsk to the Kamchatka Peninsula. With a guide, they then

Dumitru Dan and Paul Pârvu. By kind permis-
sion of the Buzau County Museum

continued in the biting conditions. Fortunately, they managed to find respite aboard a Dutch ship they had previously travelled on, before their eventual arrival in North America.

The two friends walked down the long west coast and held performances in Vancouver and San Fransisco before setting sail for Peru. Fortunately, they had been provided with free tickets.

Dumitru Dan walking, image with kind permission of the Buzau County Museum

During this part of the journey, Pârvu's legs were continually aching, which was not helped by their long days of walking. They gave a limited concert in Lima, as there were now, only two people to perform. They continued aboard another vessel, with more deck-walking, until arriving in Santiago, eventually making their way to Montevideo and Rio de Santos. The local press were again announcing the arrival of the Romanian pair who, by then, had become generally known as the 'Globetrotters'.

After free passage northwards to the United States, they made their way to Tampa City in Florida. Paul was taken into hospital where it was discovered his legs were in need of complete rest. All the years of walking had finally taken its toll. Paul insisted that Dumitru should carry-on alone. It was agreed that Paul would remain in the hospital along with their faithful dog, Harap. He sailed to a number of Caribbean Islands and to Venezuela. During a stop-off in Caracas in Venezuela, Dumitru made a telephone call to his friend Paul, and was told his condition was steadily improving with rest. However, some time afterwards, in May 1915, Paul died from an infection after having to have both of his legs amputated.

It was more times around the deck before arriving back in Europe. Dumitru walked his way through the south of Europe before his eventual arrival back in Bucharest in 1916. Unfortunately, due to the First World War, he was unable to continue to Paris to finish the global challenge. The long hike was on pause. During the remaining years of war, Dumitru volunteered to serve in the Buzau Eighth Regiment.

Eventually, in 1923, Dumitru Dan decided to finish the trek off and he walked to Paris. In doing so, he had completed the first ever global walk. He was duly named 'Champion du Monde' by the Touring Club de France. He had travelled through five continents, sailed across three oceans and walked through 74 countries!

Later years

After his global adventure, Dumitru worked firstly in Romania's Revenue and Customs Department before becoming a geography teacher. On retiring from teaching, he gave numerous talks throughout Romania where he described his globetrotting adventure. In 1936, Dumitru Dan married Adelina Negulescu and they adopted Steliana Sirbescu, Dumitru's child from a previous relationship.

He died in the city of Buzau in the south-east of Romania in 1978, aged 89. His grave and monument to his globetrotting journey can be found in the Buzau Heroes' Cemetery. Dumitru Dan's record for being the first person to walk around the world was entered into the *Guinness Book of World Records* in 1985.

In more recent years, the extensive collection of most of the certificates and artefacts from Dumitru Dan's remarkable journey have been put on display in the Buzau County Museum in Romania. Indeed, there is a large room dedicated entirely to the globetrotter's walk around the world. It is a celebration of an extraordinary man on a truly incredible journey.

Monument to Dumitru Dan in Buzau, Romania

Matthew Henson

Who was he?

Matthew Henson was an African American. From humble beginnings as both orphan and cabin boy, he became a formidable Arctic traveller who played a central role in the first expedition to the most northerly point of our planet. His understanding of survival skills learnt from the Inuit, his resourcefulness, determination and courage were impressive. Such qualities were essential in bringing success to the Robert Peary Arctic expeditions over a period of eighteen years. Matthew's extraordinary contribution to Arctic exploration, was eventually recognised as the United States gradually became to accept the place of African Americans within society.

His earlier life

Matthew was born in Maryland in the USA in 1866, a year after the end of the American Civil War. He was born on a sharecropper farm into a family with three other siblings. When he was two years of age, his mother died and a few years later, his father remarried. His childhood wasn't an easy one, with Matthew receiving considerable disruption and physical abuse. After spending three days in bed after a severe beating by his step mum, Matthew left home and found work as a kitchen helper in an eating house.

At the age of twelve, he decided to run away to sea where he began a new life as a cabin boy. On board ship the skipper, Captain Childs, took Matthew under his wing and taught him to read and write. Matthew was keen to learn about everything he saw around him. He managed to receive a wide-ranging education, mastering a number of skills and eventually became an accomplished seaman. He travelled to various regions of the world including Europe, North Africa and China. Aged 21, he was hired to work in Nicaragua by Robert Peary, an American naval commander. This work was part of a project to build a possible canal from the Atlantic to the Pacific Ocean. Peary was impressed with Henson, especially with his mechanical, navigational and carpentry skills. He discovered Matthew was a young man who was capable of working-out solutions to a whole range of problems. As a result, he became a much valued member of the team surveying the rain forests and swamps of Central America.

His earlier Arctic adventures

The Central American experience served Matthew well because in 1891, Peary invited Henson on an expedition to Greenland and Northern Canada. Matthew accepted, eager to have another chance to travel and to see another part of the world. On arriving in the far north he whole-heartedly threw himself into the expedition's challenges which lay ahead. He learnt the Inuit language and absorbed their culture, finding out how to survive in extreme Arctic conditions, how to hunt, drive husky teams and build igloos. Such knowledge would be most useful during any proposed journeys. Matthew became popular with the Inuit people; they were impressed at how he had readily adapted to their way of life. They named Matthew, Maye-Paluq, the 'kind one'. In his autobiography Matthew explained how he had come to embrace their world:

…speaking their language, dressing in the same kind of clothes, living in the same kind of dens, eating the same food, enjoying their pleasures, and frequently sharing their griefs. I had come to love these people.

The Inuit skills Matthew had absorbed, he then shared with other expedition members. Robert Peary once described Matthew as, 'more of an Inuit than many of them!' Matthew also persuaded members of the Inuit community to join them on their Arctic explorations. Using his many practical skills, he personally built each of the many sledges required for their trips across the snow and ice. Then, with a few selected American expedition members and some Inuit, a vast region of northern Canada and Greenland was explored and mapped over a number of years.

On one of their many trips, large meteorites were discovered just lying upon the snow. These were eventually taken back to the US where they were sold which, in turn, created extra funds for future Arctic exploration. On another extended journey during

Matthew with their specially designed sledges. Image by kind permission of Hodder and Stoughton

1893, to chart the ice cap, their trip almost ended in tragedy. They had run out of food and the party ended up eating all but one of their husky dogs. Another trip also ended badly when six of their Inuit team died during the trip. Extreme danger was never far away. However, their extensive exploration of the far north never revealed a hoped-for land bridge or northerly island which would have made any possible journey to the North Pole more achievable. Becoming the first to travel to the Pole had always been a dream of Robert Peary.

The North Pole

Having gained a great deal of experience in Arctic travel, Commander Peary, along with his fellow adventurer, Matthew Henson, made a number of attempts to reach the North Pole. Peary realised his companion was key to any success stating: "Henson must go with me. I cannot make it without him!" In 1900 they succeeded in travelling further north than any expedition before them. Then, in another attempt a few years later, they succeeded in getting even closer to the Pole.

Both explorers realised opportunities to reach the Pole were diminishing as they were both getting older after so many years of Arctic exploration. So in 1909, on Ellesmere Island in the north of Canada, they were ready to try again. The plan was to travel the 782 kilometres to their goal by placing caches of equipment and food along the way. These dumps of food and equipment would then be used on the journey coming back from the Pole. Twenty-four men, nineteen sledges, along with 133 dogs, were in place. Their journey involved battling with piled up sea-ice, dealing with open water, as well as surviving blizzards, the extreme cold and fatigue. It was a journey of constant danger.

Daily travel upon the sea-ice wasn't at all straightforward. Trying to take the sledges over any stacked ice would invariably slow their journey down as both dogs and humans worked hard to pull and push them over icy obstacles. These hills of ice or pressure ridges, were produced when floating ice-floes collided into each other. Sometimes the blocks of ice would be tens of metres high and would take teams a long time to make their way over them.

Similarly, finding open areas of sea-water would make their journeying difficult as they attempted to find a way around the open water or 'leads', as they are called. Sometimes the leads were so extensive the party would have no alternative but to wait until the sea froze. Alternatively, teams could travel along the edge of the ice, often adding great distances before they would be able to find a crossing point. They could then cross the thinly formed ice and continue their journey. Then, an added danger would be the risk of falling through thin ice. Indeed, this happened to Matthew on their trip northward. His life was saved by Ootah, his Inuit friend who was with him. Ootah quickly pulled him out of the water and realising Matthew's feet were in danger of being frostbitten, he placed them onto his stomach in order to warm them up! Having been in the Arctic for so many years, Matthew had watched many of the Inuit grow-up, he knew them well. Saving each other from the dangers of the Arctic, becomes second nature.

As the expedition continued moving north, some in the party, would then return, leaving only the more capable members and the strongest dogs to carry on. Matthew, so vital to the success of the expedition, continued travelling ever northward as he navigated, repaired sledges, dealt with dogs, interpreted with the Inuit and used his many other skills to keep the party moving. Finally, after 37 days, Henson, Peary and four Inuit, Ootah, Egingwah, Seegloo and Ooqueah, finally reached the North Pole! Congratulations were in order and photographs were taken. After so many years working towards this goal, they had managed to get to the very top of planet Earth. Then, they returned to Ellesmere Island. As planned, the party used the dumps of supplies strategically placed at various points on their journey back.

After the expedition
News of the expedition reaching the North Pole was somewhat

dampened by a fellow American, called Frederick Cook. He had travelled with Peary and Henson on previous Arctic journeys but hadn't been on this 1909 expedition. Cook was claiming he had reached the North Pole a year before! There were others who suggested the Peary/Henson expedition couldn't have possibly succeeded, saying they had travelled too far, too quickly and that their navigation techniques were questionable. Yet, there were others who believed the expedition was indeed the first to reach the North Pole. There was considerable debate. After investigation, it was agreed that Cook had not reached the North Pole and was completely discredited. However, continued criticism of the Peary/Henson expedition, resulted in some doubt over the success of their North Pole journey. Eventually however, the majority of people believed in the expedition's success, although there were always some who remained unconvinced.

Matthew Henson and Robert Peary's personal fortunes differed greatly on their return to the USA, during a period of extreme racial inequality. Peary enjoyed fame, received many honours and was promoted to rear admiral. However, Henson's contribution to their Arctic success was largely ignored. He struggled to find employment, eventually finding work as a clerk in a customs house. However, as societal changes gradually took place in the United States, Matthew's achievements were slowly being recognised. In 1937, years after the 1909 expedition, Matthew was finally allowed to become a member of the prestigious US Explorers' Club. Later still, in 1954 when Matthew was 88 years of age, President Eisenhower honoured him for his part in reaching the North Pole. The following year, Matthew died.

Having so many years away exploring in the far north, had led to the failure of Matthew's first marriage to Eva Flint. However, during his years in the Arctic, he had taken an Inuit partner named Akatingwah with whom he had a son, called Anauakaq. On his return to America, Matthew lost contact with his family in Greenland. However, in 1907 he married again, to a woman called Lucy Ross. In 1988, descendants of his Inuit family eventually visited

Standing at the North Pole with Matthew Henson in the middle

the United States to witness the reinterment of Matthew's body into the Arlington National Cemetery in Washington in recognition of his contribution to Arctic exploration. He was laid to rest next to Robert Peary – the two explorers together again!

Decades of dispute continued regarding whether the 1909 expedition had actually reached the North Pole. A 2005 expedition, led by Tom Avery, was prompted by this debate. The expedition decided to replicate the 1909 journey using the equipment and navigational methods used during that time. The party of five covered the same distance in 36 days 22 hours, four hours quicker than the 1909 expedition which had taken 37 days. The criticism that the 1909 time had been just too quick in reaching the North Pole, was dispelled. In their view, the 2005 team believed the Henson/Peary party, may have indeed been the first people to have journeyed to the top of the world. Both parties had been practically identical in their journey to the Pole and had almost taken the same amount of time.

The 1909 expedition was a remarkable achievement for all those involved. The skills and knowledge learnt, the determination to succeed and the courage displayed, over the many years of numerous expeditions leading up to that date, were of the highest order. And, Matthew Henson's participation in that historical journey, was so important to the expedition's success. His, is a truly inspirational story!

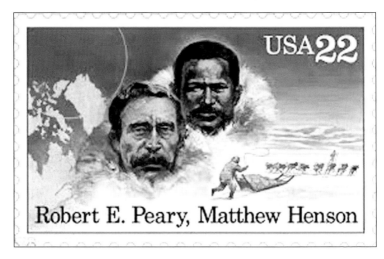

Commemorative US 22c stamp

Freda du Faur

Who was she?

In just four seasons of climbing in New Zealand between 1909-13, Freda du Faur became one of the leading female climbers in the world. With a natural gift for mountaineering, she became the

first woman to ascend Aoraki/Mount Cook and was the first person to climb all five of New Zealand's highest peaks. Amongst the mountains Freda ascended, many were previously unclimbed and others were made by new routes. She is also renown for challenging many societal conventions of the day, during a period of growing female emancipation.

Her Early Life

Emmeline Freda du Faur was born and brought up in Sydney, Australia, where she lived near to the newly created Ku-ring-gai Chase National Park. Her father was an affluent stock and land agent which enabled Freda, in her later life, to receive an independent income. As a young woman she enjoyed the solitude of bush-walking alone in the national park. There, she developed a love for both wild environments and exploration. During such jaunts she would walk through valleys with rocky outcrops running along their length, some of which would be over 100 metres in height. Lured by these lines of crags, she discovered the joy of rock climbing, as she ventured ever upwards. Sometimes she just wanted to get to the top, on other occasions she might want to look at the view or to look at some flowers growing high upon a ledge. As a consequence, she taught herself how to rock climb. Occasionally during such free-climbing exploits, Freda would face some challenging climbing problems as she scaled the rocks without any companion or rope at hand! All the time, she was honing her skills, developing her self sufficiency and a love of climbing. It became a source of pure enjoyment and freedom.

Her first visits to New Zealand

Freda's summers were mainly spent visiting New Zealand. On one trip to an art exhibition in Christchurch, she became mesmerised by images she saw of the country's Southern Alps. As she gazed at the pictures, she made a decision to go and visit these spectacular mountains so dramatically covered in snow and ice. In 1906, she journeyed to these mountains situated in the South

Peter and Alec Graham standing behind Freda du Faur.

Island. On viewing the high mountains for the first time, she became utterly captivated. She vowed there and then, to climb high up onto a mountain as far as she could and just bury her hands in the snow! She would then dig until her 'snow-starved Australian soul' was satisfied!

She returned to the mountains in 1909 and met Peter Graham, the renowned chief guide at the Hermitage, a mountain centre in the middle of the Southern Alps. He taught her how to use ropes and to climb on snow and ice. In her first season, Freda completed a series of increasingly difficult climbs, beginning with Mount Sealy and Mount Malte Brun. Peter recognised Freda's mountaineering talent straightaway, and although it was her first season of climbing in the Southern Alps, they made an attempt on the highest peak of them all – Aoraki/Mount Cook. Unfortunately, they were defeated by both large glacial crevasses and ice covered rocks high up on the mountain. Freda had obviously taken to the climbing of these high mountains. She had athleticism, endurance and competence along with a natural aptitude, all of which were so necessary in the climbing of these challenging peaks. Her years of rock climbing and walking in the Australian bush had served her well.

Climbing mountains was considered to be an unusual pastime for a woman during the early 1900s. Unfortunately, spending time alone in the mountains with a male guide caused some consternation amongst many people during these times which were awash with strict Edwardian values. Freda was warned on numerous occasions that by travelling alone in these mountains with only a single male companion, would tarnish her reputation! Was the climbing of a mere mountain, worth the risk of ruining her standing in society? Such warnings about her creating a scandal, greatly annoyed Freda. Her reply: 'I pointed out that I had come to the mountains to climb, not to sit and admire the view.'

Other people would sometimes accompany her on trips and act as chaperone, thus avoiding any possible embarrassment. If Freda could find no other visitors to go into the mountains, then

Freda climbing in the Southern Alps

taking two guides on such trips was always another solution. She did however, decide to modify her mountaineering attire in order to make it easier to climb in. Freda chose to wear a knee length skirt, knickerbockers and long 'puttees' (like gaiters). This too was considered to be quite revolutionary at a time when all ladies were expected to wear ankle-length dresses!

Looking down the Perouse Glacier.

Making history

Freda returned to New Zealand for the summer climbing season of 1910. Determined to be as fit as she could, she had spent the previous three months training at a physical education institute in Sydney. Her trainer was a woman called Muriel Cadogan, who would later become her partner. Not long after returning to the Southern Alps, Freda, Peter Graham and his brother Alec, succeeded in making an ascent of the 3754m high Aoriki/Mount Cook, which was the first ever ascent of the country's highest peak by a woman. A rope length from the summit, her guides left

Freda to climb to the top on her own.

'I gained the summit… on top of the world… I could not believe the goal I had dreamed of was beneath my feet.'

It was a significant moment in Freda's life, and of course, in the history of climbing in New Zealand. The climb was only the second ever ascent along the west ridge. The party had managed to climb to the highest point in the land, using the rudimentary equipment of the day. This didn't include the use of crampons but did require the holding of cumbersome lanterns as they climbed during the dark before dawn. It had also been the fastest ascent to that date, a staggering fourteen hours, which included a two hour stay on the summit!

Southern Alps, 1915.

That same season Freda went on to climb Mount De La Beche, Silberhorn, Mount Green and the first ascent of Mount Chudleigh. Freda had now found fame amongst the mountains, climbing to the same level as her guides in just two seasons! Her new climbing acquaintances continually talked of possible ascents they might make during these pioneering days where there was so much exploring to be made. Concerns about climbing alone with males became almost an irrelevance as she had gained mountaineering notoriety and status. Freda now pleased herself who she climbed with. She commented:

> I was the first unmarried woman to climb in New Zealand, and in consequence I received all the hard knocks until one day when I awoke more or less famous in the mountaineering world, after which I could and did do exactly as seemed to me best.

The following climbing season Freda climbed Mount Tasman, the second highest peak in the Southern Alps. She also made the first ascent of the very challenging Mount Dampier, the third highest mountain. She climbed a new route on Mount Lendenfield, and made the first ascent of Mount Du Faur (named in her honour) and Mount Nazomi.

Her fourth and final season of climbing in New Zealand was when Freda had her greatest climbing achievements. In January 1913, Freda and Peter along with another guide, David Thomson, made what is known as the 'Grand Traverse of Mount Cook', the first ever crossing of the three summits of Aoraki/Mount Cook. This classic alpine outing involved bivouacking and one epic twenty-hour climbing session! That same season, she also completed the first ever traverse of Mount Sefton in some of the most difficult mountain conditions any in her party had ever experienced. Freda also made the second ascent of Aiguilles Rouge and climbed two new peaks, which she named Mount Pibrac and Mount Cadogan (after her partner). At the end of the season, Freda bade farewell to the Southern Alps for she had made plans to travel afar.

Her later years

In 1913 Freda and Muriel Cadogan, moved to Britain, on the other side of the world. It was an opportunity to live together as a couple in a world where such relationships were considered most unacceptable. It was also part of a grand plan for Freda to climb in other parts of the world: the European Alps, Canada and perhaps the Himalaya. However, their climbing dreams were curtailed because of the outbreak of World War One. Therefore, they decided to live in London, later moving to Bournemouth. During this period, Freda worked on writing a book about her exploits in the Southern Alps.

The pair also campaigned for the suffragette movement taking place at the time. However, both women suffered from degrees of mental illness. Muriel suffered a breakdown, which led to her receiving treatment in a sanatorium. Reflecting the misguided attitudes of the time, both Muriel and Freda received treatment for being lesbian! In 1929, Muriel returned to Australia, but unfortu-

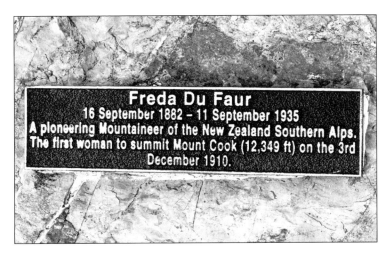

Freda du Faur's headstone in Sydney, Australia, with kind permission of Sandra Brown, Monument Australia Website

nately died of a heart attack on the journey. Some time afterwards, Freda also went back to Australia and continued bush-walking near to her home in Sydney. Not long after resuming her life back in Australia, and feeling a huge loss for her partner, Freda took her own life. She was aged 53.

For 70 years Freda lay in an unmarked grave in a cemetery in a suburb of Sydney. However, in 2006, a memorial stone was finally placed upon her grave. The ceremony included a variety of people from both Australia and New Zealand. They were there to recognise Freda's significance to mountaineering in the Southern Alps during the early 1900s. It was time to give their respects to an outstanding personality who had given so much to mountain exploration and to the reshaping of societal values of the day.

Nobu Shirase

Who was he?

Nobu Shirase was a Japanese explorer who led an expedition to the Antarctic from 1910-12. He was an adventurer who had always wanted to travel to polar regions. Against the odds, he led a Japanese expedition to Antarctica on a shoestring during a time when such trips were unheard of in Japan. Although he faced many hardships and setbacks, he

Nobu Shirase, with kind permission of the Shirase Expeditionary Memorial Museum.

managed to fulfil his childhood dream. The expedition managed to travel deep into the continent, they explored new regions and accumulated a considerable amount of scientific material.

Early Life

Nobu was born in 1861 in Konoura on Honshū Island and was the son of a buddhist priest. From the age of eight, he became intrigued by stories about explorers from around the world. In particular, he became enthralled with tales regarding polar regions. After hearing about explorers in their attempts to reach the North Pole, he decided he wanted to go there. Nobu's writing in his school journal was full of stories he had written about visits to the Arctic and Antarctic.

He was influenced by one particular teacher who taught him how to strengthen your body for living in cold places. His teacher suggested it was necessary to make five commitments to your body. These are: never drink alcohol, never smoke tobacco, never drink tea, never drink hot water and, even in cold weather, never light a fire for warmth! It is said that from a very young age, Nobu used to sleep with his bedroom windows wide open, even during wintertime. He had already decided, even at such a young age, that he was going to be a polar explorer. In 1879 he entered a school for buddhist priests but soon realised it wouldn't help him become such an adventurer, so he left.

Aged twenty, he joined the army, in the belief it would be good preparation for future polar travel. In 1883 he was posted to the disputed Kuril Islands, the sub-arctic archipelago located between northern Japan and Siberian Russia. Lieutenant Nobu was involved in the exploration of these islands over two winters, all the time learning how to live in extreme environments. Conditions were so bad that a number of fellow soldiers died. Nobu was the only person to survive scurvy out of four people. Later, he spent a year on a secret military mission in the Alaskan Arctic. There, he experienced an even tougher environment. It was so extreme, he was one of

Nobu Shirase, with kind permission of the Shirase Expeditionary Memorial Museum.

only two officers who managed to survive the trip along with a few crew.

Japanese Antarctic Expedition

During his time in the Kuril Islands, Nobu made secret plans to be the first person to travel to the North Pole. However in 1909, on hearing of the American explorer, Robert Peary's claim of reaching the North Pole, he turned his sights to the South Pole. He eventually made his ideas public and announced his intention to raise the Japanese flag at the South Pole. Although over the years, Japan had been coming out of a period of isolationism, there didn't appear to be much interest for such exploration within Japanese society. Politicians were dubious and the press and public generally mocked his idea. Consequently, Nobu had difficulties in finding any financial backing from either the government or from the public at large.

However, he did eventually manage to secure backing from Count Okuma, a former premier of Japan. Nobu set up the 'Antarctic Expedition Supporters' Association' with Okuma at its head. Gradually, funds from across Japanese society, began to trickle in. It wasn't quite the amount of money Nobu was hoping for, but it was enough to purchase a small schooner for their journey to Antarctica. They named the vessel the *Kainan Maru* translated as 'Southern Pioneer'.

Expedition members were gradually found including a ship's captain and crew, scientists, a film-maker, dog-drivers and other members who would be responsible for various aspects of the expedition. In addition, the team managed to obtain a whole range of supplies and equipment for the journey. The preparation for the trip had taken a great deal longer than Nobo had wanted. Roald Amundsen from Norway and Robert Scott from Britain, were also planning expeditions to the South Pole. They were already on their way to the Antarctic. Finally, in December 1910, the Japanese Antarctic Expedition consisting of 27 men and 30 husky dogs, left Tokyo aboard the *Kainan Maru*. There were now three expeditions bidding to be the first to the South Pole. Similar to the other two expeditions, Nobu Shirase planned to overwinter in Antarctica before pushing for the Pole the following spring.

On 7 February 1911, they arrived in Wellington Harbour in New Zealand to take-on more supplies. The Evening Post newspaper printed:

> This afternoon, the *Kainan Maru*, slight in build but big in ambition, slowly steamed into harbour... Lieutenant Shirase hopes to establish a base... for a dash to the Pole.

Those that came to view the ship, made comments regarding its size, being much smaller than both Amundsen's and Scott's vessels. Practically all of the comments which were made by visitors were extremely derogatory. Even the food they were to eat was criticised. Pemmican, which had become the staple polar food used during expeditions, a high-energy mix of meat and lard, wasn't going to be taken. Instead, the Japanese party would be having a diet of rice and plum pickles, cured beans and cuttlefish. The general consensus was that such food wasn't at all ideal food for travelling to the South Pole. After their brief stop in New Zealand,

*The Kainan Maru, with kind permission of the Shirase
Expeditionary Memorial Museum.*

they continued south through ferocious storms and hundreds of drifting icebergs, some as high as 75 metres. When they reached the Ross Sea off the coast of Antarctica, the conditions became even worse.

Due to their delay in leaving Japan and being so late in the season, they realised that any landing on the ice of the Antarctic for their overwinter camp, would be impossible. So, Nobu Shirase took the decision to turn ship and head for Australia. They were then forced to wait until the following southern summer before another attempt at landing in Antarctica. He realised this would probably end any hope of being first to the South Pole. The arrival of the *Kainan Maru* in Sydney Harbour took the inhabitants of the city by surprise. During their stay in Australia the Japanese party was accused of spying and their entire plans for polar exploration were brought into question. They were subjected to a great deal of animosity from many of the local inhabitants. In his log, Nobu wrote:

> The *New Zealand Times* was particularly poignant in its comments… that we had a crew of gorillas sailing about in a miserable whaler.

However, encouragement and assistance was offered from another polar explorer, the Australian geologist, Tennatt David who had been a member of Ernest Shackleton's 1907 Antarctic expedition. Fortunately, all the Japanese expedition members were allowed to camp in the grounds of a large house in an elegant area of the city. There, they erected their expedition prefabricated hut to live in. They lived frugally off their supplies during this enforced halt to their journey.

As the majority sat out the season, Captain Nomura took the *Kainan Maru* and sailed back to Japan with a number of his crew in an attempt to obtain extra funding and supplies. Eventually, they returned with extra supplies along with a full contingent of dogs, replacing the previous team which had all died apart from one. Just before setting off for Antarctica, Nobu Shirase presented

Tennatt David with his treasured samurai sword as a gesture of friendship. He had made the expedition's stay in Australia more tolerable after encountering the unfriendliness from the majority of their hosts.

Seven months after arriving in Sydney, on 19 November 1911, the expedition set off once more for Antarctica. Their realistically revised objective was to concentrate on carrying-out scientific measurements and a general exploration of King Edward VII Land. On entering the Ross Sea they made their way to the edge of the Ross Ice Shelf. They went alongside another ship anchored off the shelf and were amazed to learn it was Amundsen's ship *Fram*. The occupants were waiting to hear news from the South Pole.

'The Dash Patrol' where the expedition went as far as they could into Antarctica during the time they had, with kind permission of the Shirase Expeditionary Memorial Museum.

The *Kainan Maru* eventually moored beneath some sheer ninety metre high ice cliffs in the Bay of Whales. It then took some 60 hours of hard work to make a pathway up the cliff. Once on the ice, Nobu prepared for his southward dash. Having come this far, the expedition would split in two, with one group

Photograph with kind permission of the Shirase Expeditionary Memorial Museum.

exploring King Edward VII Land and the other, going inland in what they called their 'Dash Patrol'. Seven men were selected to travel southwards, two of whom would take temperature readings and other scientific measurements at base camp. The other five would take supplies of food for twenty days and head south with their dogs and sleds. In the group were two expert dog handlers, Ainu men, from the far north of Japan. As well as Nobu himself, the expedition scientist, Terutaro Takeda, would also be travelling with the team along with another member of the expedition.

Their journey began. It was a dream come true for Nobu Shirase, who since childhood, had imagined this moment. Progress was exceptionally slow due to the heavy loads being carried in the sleds and the fierce blizzards which blew day after day. Temperatures fell below -25 degrees Celsius and frostbite claimed the lives of some of the dogs.

After one week, Nobu called a halt to their journey south after calculating they only had enough food for their return journey. They had reached a point just over 80 degrees south, a distance of 257 kilometres from where they had begun. The party ceremoniously flew the Japanese flag from a bamboo pole, saluted the Emperor with three traditional Banzai (a Japanese greeting to the Emperor) before burying a record of their expedition visit inside a copper case. Their return journey lasted just three days.

Just over 80 degrees south the party ceremoniously flew the Japanese flag from a bamboo pole. Image with kind permission of the Shirase Expeditionary Memorial Museum.

At the same time, other members of the expedition surveyed the coastline further west and explored King Edward VII Land. They managed to scale an ice wall some 46 metres in height. Two men then reached the Alexandra Mountain Range which had never been seen close-up before. Crevasses and an avalanche thwarted their attempt to travel any further. They had travelled a total of sixty kilometres taking nothing with them apart from some food they could fit into their pockets and a geological hammer for collecting specimens. The ship then had difficulty in returning to the Bay of Whales because of rough seas and blizzards. When both parties were safely back on board the *Kainan Maru*, they left Antarctica.

After a brief visit to Wellington in New Zealand, in June 1912 they arrived back in Japan after sailing a total of 48,000 kilometres. There was a tumultuous celebration, with 50,000 well-wishers welcoming them home, compared with the handful that had seen them off at the start of their journey! Nobu Shirase had become a national hero.

Image with kind permission of the Shirase Expeditionary Memorial Museum.

Later life

Nobu Shirase's expedition had been very successful. Although they hadn't managed to get to the South Pole, they had been the first people from Asia to explore the Antarctic. It was an extraordinary feat: their expedition had been created on a shoestring and had no previous experience to refer to. All the members of the expedition had returned safely, no one had died or been injured and there was no damage to their ship.

Unfortunately, any fame was short lived and Nobu Shirase's expedition to Antarctica was largely forgotten. It was a regrettable fact but Nobu had to spend many years paying back huge loans which he had incurred. To help pay back these loans, he managed to sell the *Kainan Maru*. He also wrote an account of his expedition and gave many talks throughout Japan. However, Nobu had such a huge debt, he spent the rest of his life trying to pay it off.

He and his wife, Yasu, led an impoverished life in the town of Konoura, living in a rented room on the second floor above a fish shop. His diminished fortune was such that his neighbours had no idea they were living next to Japan's pioneering Antarctic explorer. He died in 1946 at the age of 85. Sadly, nobody was in attendance at his funeral.

Today, in the city of Nikaho, the Shirase Antarctic Expedition Party Memorial Museum now celebrates his pioneering expedition. Also, a Japanese Antarctic research ship and icebreaker has been named the *Shirase* in his honour. And, the east side of the Ross Ice Shelf and the Ross Sea is now known as the Shirase Coast. These are fitting dedications to Nobu Shirase and the young boy who once dreamt of exploring the polar world. After so much personnel effort over many years, this Japanese Antarctic explorer was eventually able to live his dream.

Harriet Chalmers Adams

Who was she?

Harriet Chalmers Adams was a traveller with a passion for journeying to new places, particularly those within the Spanish speaking world. Whenever she travelled to different locations, she was always keen to learn about its people and to understand their culture.

Early Life

She was born in California in 1875 and from an early age developed a love for adventure, mostly due to her extensive horse riding journeys with her father. When Harriet was just eight years old she completed a tour on horseback of the Yosemite region in California with her father. Then, at the age of fourteen, they both took to the saddle again. On this trip they spent around a year exploring the western United States all the way from Oregon to the Mexican border. Their route kept to the crest of the Sierra Nevada Mountains as much as possible. These early journeys provided the perfect apprenticeship for future adventures. Harriet received her education at home, during which time she learnt several languages including Spanish, Portuguese, German, French and Italian. As well as having an enthusiasm for a range of academic subjects, she also enjoyed physical activities where she could climb, swim and play different sports.

In 1899, Harriet married Franklin Adams, who luckily, also possessed a passion for adventure. They had their honeymoon in Mexico where they travelled widely, visiting various regions throughout the country. Most of all, the couple enjoyed looking at archaeological sites where they learnt about the culture and history of its ancient peoples. On their return to California, they made plans for an even longer and more involved journey, going even deeper into the Spanish and Portuguese speaking world.

Three year South American adventure

Franklin Adams was a mining engineer who had managed to secure a new job inspecting isolated mines in various locations all across South America. The newly-weds made plans to take full advantage of Franklin's new employment situation. The couple decided to combine those mining visits with a more general exploration of many other regions all across the continent. Harriet's ultimate aim was to then write about the experiences they had and describe the locations and the people they encountered. They also made plans to take photographs, slides and motion pictures. In these early days of photography, this involved carrying an array of quite cumbersome equipment all across South America.

So, from 1904 to 1907, they journeyed extensively throughout Central and South America travelling by horse, mule, canoe, boat and by foot. Along the way they visited regions few outsiders had ever seen before. They met with indigenous peoples and descendants of ancient civilisations, and learnt about their cultures and languages. They crossed the Andes Mountains in sometimes extremely testing weather conditions and over difficult terrain. Occasionally, mountain tracks were impassable due to the snow or fallen trees and boulders. In thickly forested areas, there was often a need to use machetes to get through thick undergrowth. As well as Harriet and Frank travelling from one location to another, there were often others they met along the way, wishing to journey to similar places. And, if they were lucky enough to find one, a local guide might go along with them. If there was no guide available,

Harriet in Mongolia.

they would attempt to make their own way, deciphering often inaccurately drawn maps or verbal directions. Each night, they would stop wherever they could, sometimes sleeping out in the open or in local dwellings. During this part of their journey, Harriet and Frank covered over 1,600 kilometres on horseback. In her notes Harriet commented:

> I've wondered why men have absolutely monopolised the field of exploration... I've never found my sex a hinderment; never faced a difficulty which a woman, as well as a man, could not surmount; never felt a fear of danger; never lacked courage to protect myself. I've been in tight places and have seen harrowing things.

On their way back to the Peruvian coast, they decided to ascend El Misti, a 5,822 metres high volcano. Harriet was the first woman to have ever completed the climb.

For the next stage of their journey, they boarded a ship and headed southward along the coast of Chile, then on through the Strait of Magellan to Buenos Aires. Sailing on such wild and volatile seas around the southern tip of South America, awoke Harriet's continual problem whenever she sailed upon the open ocean: that of sea-sickness. Sailing back to Patagonia in the far south of Argentina, they then rode horses northwards across the entire length of the country. Harriet was shocked by the continuous wind which blew, '…as I have never seen it blow anywhere else in my life.'

They then spent three months in the Amazon rainforest canoeing or walking to remote villages. In these isolated locations, they met a variety of local people and learnt how it was possible to live in harmony within their environment. It was whilst travelling in the north of Brazil that Harriet came very close to death. The

Riding through the Dominican Republic.

frightening event took place after eating a forest fowl that had been killed by a poisoned arrow during a hunting trip with forest dwellers they were visiting.

During their three year journey, the couple often found themselves having very difficult days where they encountered torrential rain, blizzards, floods, altitude sickness, illness, and a loss of their pack animals and possessions. They had crossed the Andes four times on horseback and had managed to visit every country on the South American continent. It was time to head home.

Further adventures

Returning to the United States, Harriet began giving public presentations about her South American adventure. These she illustrated with her own slides and motion pictures. She also began writing articles for a variety of publications including the magazine, *National Geographic*. A key message Harriet presented to audiences was: although she was a woman, it didn't hinder her ability to explore and take part in adventures. Both her writing and lectures also challenged anti-hispanic sentiments often prevalent within the United States. This she attempted to do by portraying the people she had met as positively as she could. Harriet lectured all across the country and was considered an expert on both Central and South America. Payment for both her lectures and article writing helped finance future trips.

In order to obtain a greater understanding of the Spanish speaking world, Harriet wanted to visit all the countries in the world with either a Spanish or Portuguese connection. During 1910, the couple went on another challenging journey by following the route of Christopher Columbus across the Caribbean. Part of the trip included a difficult 800 kilometres on horseback crossing the interior of both Haiti and the Dominican Republic.

A few more journeys were made together, but on many occasions, due to Fracklin's work commitments, Harriet would travel alone. She visited various parts of Europe, North Africa, China, Mongolia, Japan, the Gobi Desert, Siberia and East Africa. Harriet often had particular objectives when visiting new locations, often gathering material for future articles and lectures. However, there was one mystery Harriet continually tried to shine some light upon. This was to try and obtain a greater understanding as to where Native Americans had originally come from. Her many

Harriet with a French soldier while working as a First World War correspondent

travels included living for three months with an indigenous group in the Philippines who were transitioning from a traditional head-hunting to a more main-stream lifestyle.

Later years

Harriet continued to travel, write and encourage others, particularly women, to explore and journey to all corners of the planet. Given her experiences in dangerous locations, she was given special permission to report from the front-line during the First World War. Indeed, she was the only female correspondent allowed by the French authorities during that war. She managed to spend time on the front line, talking to soldiers and taking photographs during which, German shells sometimes rained-down from above. On her return to the United States she wrote about the war, gave lectures and raised funds for the war effort.

Whilst in Spain in 1926, Harriet suffered a near fatal cliff-fall and was told she would never walk again. However, through utter determination, by 1929 she was both walking and travelling again. In 1934, on Franklin's retirement, the couple moved to Spain where they decided to base themselves for any future travels.

After a prolonged illness, Harriet died in Nice in 1937 at the age of 62. Over the years, Harriet has been an inspiration to many and has been referred to as 'America's greatest woman explorer.'

Geoffrey Winthrop Young

Who was he?

Geoffrey Winthrop Young was a British mountaineer, writer and educator. During his lifetime he completed a number of daring mountain ascents. He was once considered to be one of the best mountaineers of his time. In his later years, he played a key role in the creation of schemes and institutions designed to help in the development of mountaineering and outdoor pursuits.

Early Life

Geoffrey was born in 1876 in London and brought-up in Berkshire. He was from a privileged background: his father, Sir George, had been a charity commissioner, and his mother, Alice Eacy, was from an established Irish family. Geoffrey went to Marlborough School and then to Trinity College in Cambridge. As a child, his father had introduced him to mountain walking in Wales, Germany and Ireland.

Mountaineering

It was during his long summer vacation in 1896, that Geoffrey started rock-climbing. Using a hemp rope and wearing nailed boots, he completed a number of routes in the Lake District. The act of climbing, quite literally, changed his life. Whilst studying at Cambridge, a select group of students, with Geoffrey at its heart, began climbing walls, roofs and spires throughout the university. This activity was largely carried-out at nighttime because it was frowned upon by the authorities. Geoffrey even went to the trouble of producing a guidebook of the various routes he and his fellow enthusiasts enjoyed climbing in Cambridge, which was entitled: *Wall and Roof Climbing*.

During his summer vacation, Geoffrey travelled to the Alps where he completed a number of ascents of mountains during, what was still, in the relatively early days of climbing. At the end of his trip he concluded: 'I felt that I belonged to these mountains and that they belonged to me.'

Geoffrey left Cambridge in 1898 and for the next few years he lived nearer to the Alps where he studied German and French at Jena University in Germany and Geneva in Switzerland. After that, he taught at Eton School between 1900 and 1905. Throughout this period, he gained a reputation for being a talented and formidable Alpine mountaineer. Geoffrey had a vast number of friends and acquaintances he would climb with, both in the Alps and in Britain. Each year, there would be groups of people visiting certain locations where they would walk and climb. Their calendar of meets included large Easter gatherings at Snowdonia's Pen-y-Pass hotel where the entire place would be taken over by Geoffrey's friends. These informal meetings beneath Snowdon took place for over thirty years.

In the Alps, he made ascents of many of the major peaks, a number of which were new routes. The summits he climbed, amongst many others, included the Breithorn, Gspaltenhorn, Weisshorn, Täschhorn, Aiguille du Grépon, Mont Blanc and Grandes Jorasses. Geoffrey kept a journal of his mountain exploits; summing-up his 1906 Alpine season, he wrote:

Unique season – new climbs on Breithorn, Dom, Täschhorn, Weisshorn, etc. Week at Montenvert; 21 hours on Requin by wrong route, two Drus, circuit of Grépon, Charmoz and Blaitières in one day. Täschorn with Ryan, and did not expect for about six hours to get back alive.

On another occasion, he was climbing on his favourite Alpine mountain, the Weisshorn with his guide friend, Josef Knubel. Geoffrey was surprised when he realised that one of the Weisshorn ridges he had previously made a first ascent on, had been named the Young Arête in his honour!

The Weisshorn.

Having left his teaching post at Eton, in 1905, Geoffrey began a new job as one of His Majesty's Inspectors for Secondary Schools. The post was an influential job where he had considerable powers to investigate and, if required, make suggestions for school improvements. In 1907, he was elected onto the committee of the British Alpine Club; he was already a member of the Climbers' Club. One idea which Geoffrey pushed forward was for the publication of local climbing guides. Rock-climbing had become more popular on crags throughout the country. Enthusiasts went out and began climbing routes up rock faces, sometimes without any guidance or knowledge of what lay ahead.

Unfortunately, there had been a number of fatal accidents in both Wales and the Lake District. He was convinced that producing guidebooks with route descriptions and details of their difficulties and dangers, would result in fewer accidents. In 1909, a suitable climbing guide was published for Llewedd in Snowdonia, which was followed by other guides throughout various climbing regions across the country. Over the years, as Geoffrey had suggested, guidebooks have regularly been updated to allow for any revisions and to add any new climbs.

As the First World War approached, worries about the future abounded throughout Europe. Geoffrey made a quick journey to the Alps, not knowing when he would next be able to return. With two guide friends, he climbed the Zmutt Ridge on the Matterhorn. Illustrating his high level of mountaineering ability he had attained, he described his journey:

> Up the snow-covered crags of the ridge to the summit we all went separately for greater speed; and still unroped we raced down the eastern shoulder to Zermatt, beating the return rush of the snow-blizzard up the valley by a few minutes.

To be able to confidently, quickly and safely climb down the mountain unroped, obviously required considerable mountaineering ability.

A Change of Life

At the outbreak of hostilities, at the age of 38, Geoffrey was considered to be too old for military action. Instead, he became a war correspondent for the *Daily News*. He immediately sailed across the English Channel and travelled across northern France and Belgium observing, gathering information and posting reports back to London. His task was certainly helped in being fluent in both French and German.

However, with a desire to 'do better for the wounded in the war,' Geoffrey relinquished his job with the newspaper and joined a newly formed Friends' Ambulance Unit. He became a key member and helped organise the evacuation and treatment of casualties from battle zones. For months Geoffrey and his unit, saved thousands of both military and civilian lives. Risking their own safety, the ambulance unit transported them to field hospitals and to relative safety, in the Ypres area of Belgium.

In 1915, Geoffrey became a commander on the front-line for a similar ambulance unit on the Italian-Austrian front. He was the ideal person to work in such desperate situations: capable of working in dangerous and stressful circumstances; able to think clearly; and, in having a calm, tireless, decisive and authoritative disposition. In his journal he kept at the time, during one very busy week, his ambulances dealt with 1,100 stretcher cases, 1,300 other wounded cases and covered some 19,000 kilometres. Unfortunately, in the August of 1917, Geoffrey was seriously hurt by an exploding shell during the Battle of Monte San Gabriela. His injuries resulted in having his leg amputated. Not long after the operation, he managed to hobble some 25 kilometres to avoid being captured by the Austrians.

At the end of the First World War, for his bravery, Geoffery was awarded the Belgium Order of Leopold for 'exceptional courage and resource'. And, for his work on the Italian front, he was presented with the Italian Silver Medal for Valour.

Although Geoffrey had had a secret homosexual past, after the war, Geoffrey married Eleanor Slingsby whom he had known for many years. The newly married couple enjoyed many years of happiness after the horrors of the First World War. The couple had a son Jocelin, born in 1919, and a girl, Marcia, born in 1925. Geoffrey continued to write, as he had done earlier in his life, writing articles for both magazines and newspapers. Geoffrey worked on several books about aspects of mountaineering and he also wrote books of poetry.

He began climbing again during the resumption of the Easter 'Pen-y-Pass' gathering with his friends. Using his strong upper body and being protected by ropes from above and below, he climbed the rock-climbing route, Gashed Crag, on Tryfan. He designed a range of false legs with detachable feet which he could then use on different terrain: a rubber pad for walking, a ski-ring fitment for snow, and a steel spike studded with nails for rock climbing. Having to start climbing again with only one leg, required working out new ways to balance, to modify his climbing technique and realise his limitations. Cecil Slingsby, his father-in-law, described Geoffrey climbing:

> I never saw such a magnificent mountaineering feat in my life… GWY had to do practically the whole of his climbing with his hands and one foot, the right. Where nature had provided a little foot-hold for the left foot, GWY… hopped up and across with his right foot to the foot-hold designed for the left… He never grumbled, but really enjoyed himself.

In 1927, at the age of 51, Geoffrey returned to Zermatt to climb the Monte Rosa, the highest mountain in the Swiss Alps. With a strong support team around him, by moving slowly, occasionally crawling and by using a ski contraption in descent, it took a total of eighteen hours to complete his one-legged ascent. The following year, he climbed the Wellenkuppe and almost managed to climb his favourite mountain, the Weisshorn, before running out of time. Following that, Geoffrey decided to climb the Matterhorn. He believed by climbing this most famous of mountains, he would hopefully motivate others who had lost limbs, to overcome their own 'personal mountains' of adaptation and changed lives. He wrote:

> …we set off at 10:00 pm… Awkward climbing when one couldn't see the holds, especially for my left foot. But Schenton secured us ahead… and Hans… close behind… gave me a hand, knee or shoulder… for hours, placing my left foot with his hand on the holds, neatly as moving a pawn at chess.

They reached the summit by 7:30 am where they stayed for an hour. The party then began their careful and slow descent and were back down by 4:00 pm. Geoffrey had been correct about the

Geoffrey with his wife, Eleanor… and his false leg.

Matterhorn climb because the newspapers had full reports of his intrepid ascent. As a result, he then spent the next few months replying to others who had contacted him about their own problems with lost limbs.

During the 1920s Geoffrey had several mountain books published, including *Mountain Craft* a 300 page publication about the principles of mountaineering. This textbook of climbing included chapters on leadership, equipment, rock climbing and ice and snow craft. It was a comprehensive manual, quite unique for its time, which one person described as being a 'a standard, so long as mankind is interested in mountaineering.'

Around this time, Geoffery became the Consultant in the Humanities for the Rockerfeller Foundation. With his headquarters in Paris, he became involved in providing financial support for humanitarian projects in post-war Europe. He was also helping develop a new type of school with a major emphasis on young people experiencing adventurous activities. The idea was the brain-child of his close-friend, a German called Kurt Hahn, who eventually fled the tyranny of Nazis Germany in 1933 and moved to Britain. 'Gordanstoun School' was the result of their design and opened in Scotland in 1934. Geoffrey provided support over many years. It was an altogether worrying time for him as he watched Germany develop its Nazis ideology. During his visits to Germany, he provided help and encouragement, sometimes secretly, to more liberal minded Germans who were opposed to the Nazi movement. Indeed, notable individuals, including Geoffery, sent Hitler an appeal to stop the brutality within concentration camps which were being used during the 1930s.

Geoffrey continued to visit the mountains whenever he could, and with his many friends they continued to walk and climb. In 1935, Geoffrey made his last major climb in the Alps on the Zinalrothorn above Zermatt in Switzerland. It took a great deal of effort and strength to gain the summit with his party. After resting at the top, they began their descent, during which Geoffrey fell some 24 metres. In order to resume their journey, it took a huge effort to haul him back up from where he had fallen. Once safely down they were all exhausted, as they had been on the go for a total of 26 hours!

Later Years

Although Geoffrey's major mountain days were over, he continued working for the development of mountaineering and outdoor pursuits. Between 1941 to 1943, he became President of the Alpine Club, which Geof-

frey saw as an opportunity to make changes within the climbing world. One idea he worked towards was for the formation of a body which would represent the interests of climbing clubs and mountaineering in general. This culminated in the 1944 formation of the British Mountaineering Council. Also, by working alongside, Kurt Hahn, they continued to develop the concept of providing adventurous activities within educational establishments. This eventually led to the launch of the 'Outward Bound' movement, and later on, in the setting-up of the 'Duke of Edinburgh Award.'

Geoffrey died in September 1958 at the age of 82. He was once asked about the words he would like on his memorial tablet after his death. His chosen words included:

'Live life at the full. Blend dream with the deed.'

Such an epitaph perfectly describes the life story of this extraordinary man.

Millican Dalton

Who was he?

Millican Dalton was a British adventurer who, during the early 1900s, introduced a great number of people to a variety of outdoor experiences in the English Lake District and beyond. He was an original thinker and challenged conventional ideas whilst living a self-sufficient life in the open-air. He became known as the Professor of Adventure.

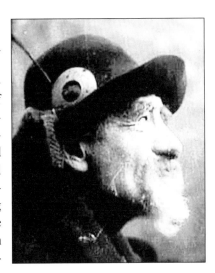

Early Life

Millican was born into a Cumberland family in 1867, one of seven children. His father worked in the lead smelting industry at Alston but unfortunately died when Millican was aged only seven. The family then moved to north London joining other extended-family members who had already moved there. An over-riding reason for many to move away from the Alston area in Cumberland was the general decline in the lead smelting industry. However, Millican and his brother, Henry, continued to attend a Quaker boarding school in the county, only visiting the rest of his family in London during holiday times.

In 1880, they left their school in the north of England and permanently moved to the capital city. However, the Dalton family didn't stay long in urban and smog filled London. They went in

187

search of a cleaner environment and moved to Essex. From a very early age, Millican enjoyed being in the wild outdoors and particularly revelled in any daring escapades. Once, after acquiring a length of rope, he constructed a rope ladder for the children to use to get in and out of the house – via his bedroom window! The children all became masterful at climbing trees, invariably being led by Millican; all these danger-filled capers were the bane of the local parents. He and Henry, began to think of even greater adventures further afield. After obtaining a tent, they would spend their weekends in Epping Forest on the outskirts of London, camping and tree climbing in all weathers.

Eventually, as it happens to us all, the carefree days of youth caught up with Millican. It was time for him to find a job. For a free-spirited, outdoor enthusiast who loved camping, climbing up trees and having adventures, what could Millican do? Answer: to secure employment as an insurance clerk in the very heart of the City of London. Although his work was somewhat stifling, at least his wages were quite good. Therefore, whenever the opportunity arose, especially during holiday times, he could go off and find adventure. With his brother, they would camp further afield in Wales, Scotland and the Lake District. Onto their bicycles they would lash heavy tents and camping gear and head off to the hills. With such hefty loads, the journeys would take a long time to cycle or sometimes push, when the terrain became too steep to negotiate. During the 1880s, in a bid to have lighter gear, Millican and Henry began to modify their camping equipment, in an attempt to travel lightly during camping trips.

However, there was a problem… increasingly, Millican was finding that his working life in the City was interfering too much with where his heart was in the wild of the outdoors. He partially overcame this dilemma by moving onto a plot of land situated in the countryside outside London. After work he could then escape to his tent. But, this still wasn't enough. Therefore, in 1904, at the age of 36, Millican gave up his clerk's life in London so he could live permanently in the outdoors. He took the decision to become self sufficient and live a simple life with nature. Matthew Entwistle, who wrote a biography of Millican Dalton, summed-up Millican's thinking at the time: 'Millican became engrossed in the outdoor scene and felt that work was beginning to interfere with leisure.'

'Professor of Adventure'

Beginning a new life in the wild, Millican decided to work on an idea he had been dreaming about for some time: he would become a mountain guide. Millican decided to use the title of Professor of Adventure and began offering his services as a guide to anybody who wished to sample the delights of an outdoor life. This would be an opportunity for those wanting to escape the humdrum life of the rat race and conventional lifestyle. The location for his new guiding service was going to be in the Lake District. His chosen base was on the fell-side, beneath crags, overlooking Derwent Water in the Borrowdale valley. There, he would erect tents for

Millican Dalton in action, image courtesy of 'Millican Dalton – A Search For Romance and Freedom' by Matthew Entwistle.

his clients during the summer. He offered a range of activities on the high fells and in lakes, rivers and streams. These adventure holidays were kept at a minimal cost by living under canvas and eating only basic but wholesome food. They were open to all, including mixed sex groups, with an emphasis on getting close to nature. Millican became well known for these adventurous holidays in the Lake District. He placed advertisements around Keswick and local photographers made a series of action postcards to promote his work.

Summer after summer, numerous groups of young and old, male and female, from many walks of life, would experience Millican's idiosyncratic adventure experiences. His programmes would be full and varied with opportunities to digress as the weather or circumstances dictated. These were action-packed days of walking, climbing and travelling upon water, and were all fuelled by their guide's very individual and original take on life. There would be treks up onto the high fells, rock climbing tuition, scrambles up active streams, canoeing or sailing on Derwent Water and the making of rafts and then trying them out.

The camps might well require exploring underground, picnicking, wild bathing, dangling off ropes or bivouacking. Cooking was communal and done on an open fire where fruit, nuts and edible plants, foraged during the day, might be cooked and eaten along with Millican's own wholemeal bread. It was a unique, well conceived programme by a man who was a true connoisseur of exciting Lake District activities. Over time, Millican led guided trips further afield to Wales, Scotland, Ireland and even to the Swiss Alps.

During wintertime, Millican would go back to the south of England, to his hut in the Epping Forest. He could then be near to his family, waiting-out the winter in relatively milder weather and in the shelter of his hut. If it snowed in the forest, he might go skating using his hand-made skates upon frozen ponds. As an alternative, he could always go off skiing on his hand-made skis. He could also complete other worthwhile activities including the

Millican Dalton, image courtesy of 'Millican Dalton – A Search For Romance and Freedom' by Matthew Entwistle.

making of his personally designed camping equipment. Having a wealth of knowledge of what works best whilst camping, he set

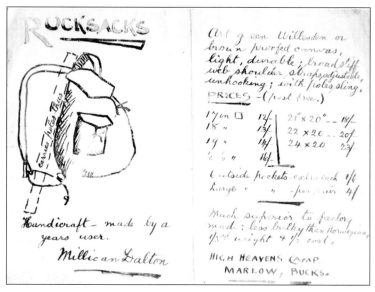

Prices for his rucksacks Millican made, image courtesy of Matthew Entwistle's book 'Millican Dalton – A Search For Romance and Freedom'.

about making tents, sleeping bags and unframed rucksacks during the winter months. These he would then sell or might hire-out to his clients during the summer.

Millican was a talented rock climber and became part of the local pioneering climbing fraternity exploring new routes in the Lake District with other like-minded pioneers of the day. He was a very good, safe, methodical climber who had an eye for an exciting route up a rock-face. Millican spent a great deal of his time just wandering around fell-side crags, looking for rocks to climb. As was his philosophy, he just climbed for the enjoyment he found. His skills and temperament made him an ideal climbing guide: he took no unnecessary risks, was very patient, was a natural teacher and, above all, he was very skilled and knowledgeable at his trade. His favourite rock climb in the Lakes was the single, pointed tooth of rock, Napes Needle on the side of Great Gable. On his fiftieth ascent, he took firewood, a kettle and water with him to have a celebratory brew at the top. Quite a feat, given the limited space on top of the Needle!

Millican Dalton's Cave

Around 1914, Millican began using a disused quarried cave at Castle Crag in Borrowdale as an alternative base for his guiding. He named it his 'Cave Hotel'. His new dwelling consisted of a general living area and a higher one for sleeping in what he called 'The Attic'. He found that his new accommodation was more sheltered, spacious and easier to live in than a tent. A feature of his new abode was that it always had a constant supply of water from the many drips from the cracks in the roof.

Millican was a great recycler and made use of discarded items

Inside Millican Dalton's Cave, Borrowdale, image by author.

from the nearby village tips. Consequently, his cave became adorned with useful objects which he had adapted to use for his every day living in his cave. Old barrels captured water dripping from the roof, he made use of crates for storing odd items and he used planks of wood for shelving. A fire was nearly always burning for cooking and for keeping the chill away, especially at night when people would gather. Millican always had an ample supply of wood, from different trees, ready to be used. He was an expert on which trees to burn for different situations. He slept on a bed of bracken and would often lay awake listening to the sounds of the fells: the wind and the many Lakeland creatures. Outside the cave, he even planted potatoes on small terraces.

Along with making his own camping equipment, Millican also made his own clothes. He always wore the same outfit which consisted of homemade shorts, his feathered Tyrollean hat, a jacket of his own design, perhaps a plaid, nailed climbing boots (without socks) and puttees. Millican was quite famous throughout the Lake District for his eccentricity. Although he stuck to a healthy

Rafting, image courtesy of Keswick Tourism Association.

diet and was a teetotaller, he constantly drank exceedingly strong coffee and he chain smoked. He was famous for always having a Woodbine cigarette in his mouth.

Millican was a very sociable person and liked nothing better than to have long discussions around campfires with his guests. The topic of conversation ranged from current affairs, politics, religion, philosophy, nature and rock-climbing. Occasionally, conversations would become extremely heated and become raging arguments. One such discussion became so acute that somebody took the trouble to carve these words into the rock just outside the cave: 'Don't waste words, jump to conclusions!'

Despite his unusual lifestyle, Millican was held in high regard by the local inhabitants of Borrowdale he came in contact with. Millican would always enjoy a chat with all he met. Although he never married, Millican enjoyed female company and, being ahead of his time, treated them as equals during any adventures. Whenever possible, Millican always encouraged girls and women he was guiding, to lead a rock-climb. He maintained lifelong beliefs which often went against mainstream thinking; he was both a socialist and a pacifist. During the Second World War he was so incensed, that he once wrote to Winston Churchill demanding an end to the fighting. In his letter, he complained that the war was interfering with his freedom, as he was being ordered by the local air raid warden to stop burning candles in his cave at night!

Later Years

He continued to spend each summer guiding groups from his Lake District cave and living wild in all weathers, both in his cave and sometimes out on the fell-side. Then, as he had done during every wintertime, he would travel south to over-winter in his hut. From 1929 onwards, Millican had re-located his winter-months' base to a plot of land in the Chiltern Hills.

Even in his seventies, he remained fit and agile and could still wander across the fells and lead people on daring trips. As always, during the winter of 1946-47, he once again travelled south to his

*Millican outside a shop reading a newspaper, image courtesy of
Keswick Tourism Association.*

hut. However, this particular winter season was a harsh one in which Millican's wooden hut unfortunately burnt down. He was therefore forced to spend the remainder of the extremely cold winter under canvas. Unfortunately, due to the constantly freezing conditions, he became ill and had to go to hospital. Whilst there, Millican caught pneumonia and suffered from heart failure. He died in the February of 1947, at the age of 79.

Millican's close friend, Mabel Barker, wrote an obituary following his death:

His picturesque figure and lovable personality have surely become part of the heritage of Lakeland... I wonder how many owed to him their first thrills on rock and rope; in camp and caves in all weathers; in forest and on water, and in the cunning management of wood fires...

Today, when people trek up to Millican's Cave by the side of Castle Crag in Borrowdale in the Lake District, visitors can appreciate the unique atmosphere of his Cave Hotel. Just like the chiselled comments upon the rocks made during his many fire-side debates, Millican Dalton's memory has been permanently etched into Lake District legend.

Gleb Travin

Who was he?

Gleb Travin cycled alone around the entire perimeter of the vast
Soviet Union between 1928 and 1931 using a basic 1920s bicycle.
He covered approximately 30,000 kilometres across some of the
world's toughest and most inhospitable landscapes. His adventure
is a story of courage, physical strength and determination. He possessed a staggering aptitude for surviving life-threatening situations in some of the most severe conditions on the planet.

His early life

Gleb was born in 1902 and grew up in Pskov in the west of Russia. As a child, his father taught him outdoor survival skills. He learnt how to forage for food, find shelter, how to hunt and eat what he caught raw. After meeting a Dutchman who was cycling around Europe, Gleb decided that one day, he too would have a similar adventure. Therefore, during his younger years, he took to riding a bicycle around the Pskov region. Being gifted in a range of physical activities, during his military service, he joined a special sports unit. He was based in Leningrad and received instruction in a host of academic subjects, as well as taking part in a range of physical activities. On being discharged from the army, he moved to the Kamchatka Peninsula in the far east of the USSR. It was there, whilst working as an electrician, he helped construct the region's first ever power station. In his free time Gleb continued to train on his bicycle. Finally, he believed he was ready for his longed-for cycling trip: he had decided to travel around the border of the Soviet Union, the largest country in the world.

Cycling along the southern border

His expedition gained approval from the authorities because they believed his trip would be an opportunity to promote sport throughout the Soviet Union. His plan was to travel on his own and rely entirely on his survival skills. Gleb was asked to keep a log-book regularly stamped during his journey, as proof of his visits to so many locations. His journey began by travelling by ship from the Kamchatka Peninsular to Vladivostok. Then, he began his long cycle-ride towards the west, along paths, forest trails and by following railway tracks. He took along with him some basic equipment and mainly ate what he could gather or hunt along the way. Whenever he could, he also ate and slept in local inhabitants' cottages.

In Siberia, the onslaught of a severe winter made the riding of his bicycle very difficult in the extreme cold and in deep snow. Now was the moment for all his gained knowledge and his instinct for survival, to come to the fore. On reaching massive Lake Baikal, he cycled across it on the thick ice. Compared to the rough undulating terrain he had been travelling over, riding across this relatively flat frozen surface was straightforward. After crossing the lake, wherever possible, he cycled along frozen river beds and lakes as the very low temperatures turned these waterways into winter highways. People along his route began to talk about the strange man upon an even stranger beast. They described the man as having an 'iron hoop' around his head! Gleb had taken to wearing a varnished strap on his head for the purpose of holding back his long hair from falling into his eyes. He had vowed not to cut his hair until his epic journey had been completed.

Weeks later, as Gleb entered the Soviet desert regions in Central Asia, it was no longer the cold but the extreme heat which was creating problems. There was a lack of both water and food, and his wheels continually sank into sand. However, he found the local people very friendly but inquisitive as to what he was actually doing on this metal machine. Many people throughout his entire journey around the border of the Soviet Union had never seen a bicycle before. During this section of his trip, Gleb was attacked by a pack of jackals and only escaped after he threatened the creatures with a burning log he had grabbed from his camp fire. He began to realise that by having a bicycle with him, tended to ward-off the majority of wild creatures. At one point, he was conscious of a tiger following him close by. But, because he had his 'strange machine' with him, the tiger had not attacked. This, he was grateful for because, at that time, he wasn't carrying a gun. 'The bike was my trusted bodyguard!' he claimed.

Eventually he reached the shores of the Caspian Sea which he crossed by ferry. On entering the high mountainous region of the Caucasus, he found himself cycling up some extreme slopes. This was extremely challenging because Gleb's machine only had a single gear, therefore a considerable amount of bike-pushing took place. After the mountains, the cycling became easier and eventually he reached Moscow.

Gleb Travin, from a painting by Nikolay Lobzov, courtesy and copyright of the artist Nikolay Lobzov.

Cycling in the Arctic

From the Soviet capital Gleb went back to where he had grown-up in Pskov. From there, he rode to Leningrad which he reached in the October of 1929, exactly one year since starting his journey. He continued on his journey to Murmansk on the Arctic coast. News of Gleb's arrival had proceeded him. He was met by a doctor who insisted on giving him a medical and was impressed at the good health Gleb was in. He bought some provisions which included warmer clothes. He also studied maps for what would be the greatest challenge of his expedition: the Soviet Arctic.

He cycled to Archangel, where he purchased a rifle, and then to Perchora and Dikson. Gleb found the conditions for cycling increasingly challenging: he was continually being slowed down by strong polar winds and deep snow. Gleb developed a routine of eating twice every day, cycling for eight hours then spending time

Gleb Travin on his journey.

finding food to eat. He would shoot wild creatures (arctic fox, seal, walrus) and catch fish, all of which, he mostly ate raw. He often sought the advice of local nomadic people he met along the way as to the best routes to take. Gleb developed a fondness for the traditional peoples he met as he travelled through the Arctic. Despite the incredibly challenging conditions day after day in such extreme terrain, he actually enjoyed being in the far north. He liked the beauty of this frozen world: 'It fills me with joy and strength,' he once said.

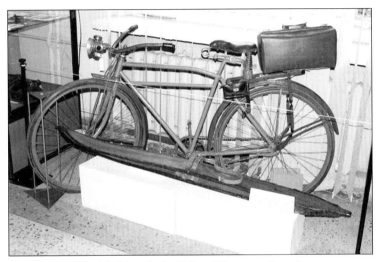

Gleb's bicycle in Pskov Museum, Russia.

Gleb discovered he could travel most quickly whenever he cycled over the relatively flat snowy surfaces of the frozen sea. He constructed shelters for his overnight stops, by chopping-out ice blocks. He made a habit of placing his bike facing southwards so he would be correctly orientated the following day. However, one day, the wind was so strong that both Gleb and his bicycle were just being blown across the surface of the snow and ice. Using his knife, he managed to make himself a small ice shelter as the wild wind continued to blow throughout the day and on into the night.

Come the next morning, Gleb realised he was suffering from frostbite.

He tried breaking free from the ice and snow all around him. Managing to extricate both himself and his cycle, which was also solidly frozen into the icy surface, he staggered off. He walked a considerable distance before spotting a sledge track which eventually led him to a traditional nomadic tent. The occupants were shocked in seeing what a terrible state the stranger was in. He was given shelter, a warm drink and some food. Gleb started to really suffer from the frostbite: extreme pain began and the infected parts began to swell. Some time later, he decided to act.

The hut's occupants were aghast as they watched Gleb cut-off certain parts of his toes before any gangrene set-in, removing infected skin with his own knife. In a weakened state, he decided to continue his journey. As he camped-out the next evening, Gleb was then attacked by an arctic fox. Sensing Gleb's weakness, the fox tried to steal some food he was eating. There ensued a tussle in the snow where, eventually, the fox came-off worse. Some time after that, he took shelter on the icebreaker ship *Lenin* which had stopped off shore in the ice in the Kara Sea. As the vessel remained locked in the ice, it was an opportunity to recuperate from his ordeal.

In October 1930, Gleb attempted crossing the Pyasina, the largest river on the Taimyr Peninsular. The river had only just started to freeze over. Ice lay thin and was slippery to ride upon. Suddenly, as he was nearing the opposite shore, he fell from his bike and broke through the ice. Gleb found it difficult to escape from the ice, finding it necessary to spread-eagle his weight. Moving like a seal, he slowly shuffled himself and his machine to the shore. Eventually, he managed to warm himself by getting in amongst a tall pile of recently skinned reindeer hides. The following day, he came across the owner of the skins who was out with his dog team. The man gave Gleb a lift upon his sled and told him the best route to continue his journey.

It took two months of exceedingly difficult travelling to cross the massive Taymyr Peninsular. He reached a village inhabited by a community of Russian settlers on the Indigirka River. Gleb decided to stay for a while and was treated well as their guest. It was another opportunity to recuperate from yet another injury after an ice-cave he had been sleeping in had collapsed. During his stay he helped teach children in their small school where he told them many stories about his adventures.

Gleb pressed on in the severe cold and ferocious weather, across the vast, barren and ice strewn Arctic landscape. In Chukotka, in the remote north-east of the country, Gleb killed a polar bear for food. However, he hadn't noticed there was a cub nearby; for many weeks afterwards, the cub, which he named Mishutka, followed him. Gleb and the cub ate together and sheltered at the same location overnight. On reaching the settlement of Pevek, Gleb left Mishutka behind at the trading centre there. Eventually, Gleb arrived in the far north-eastern corner of the Soviet Union at Cape Dezhnev and the town of Uelen. From there he completed his ground-breaking journey by boarding a ship back to Kamchatka. Gleb had achieved the impossible – he had journeyed around the perimeter of the Soviet Union on a bicycle!

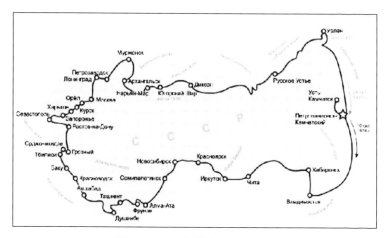

The route of Gleb's journey.

Later in life

After his incredible journey, Gleb settled in Kamchatka and became a sports instructor and taught military sciences. He also found work as an electrician. During World War Two he became a military instructor and a commander of a coastal defence regiment. Gleb's bicycle and some of the artefacts from his journey are on display in the Pskov Museum in western Russia. Gleb Travin died in 1979 at the age of seventy-seven.

After his momentous journey had been completed, Gleb revealed his philosophy about what it had been like during his bicycle trip around the Soviet Union: 'Every day I took an examination. If I passed, I would remain alive. To fail – meant death.'

His journey has to be one of the most incredible adventure stories in recent history. An absolutely remarkable feat.

*I must thank Andrey Baydin for his assistance
with the research for this chapter.*

Kazimierz Nowak

Who was he?

Kazimierz Nowak was a courageous and resourceful Polish adventurer, journalist and photographer. He successfully travelled overland and alone across the length of a wild and dangerous 1930s Africa. His journey was fraught with many dangers and difficulties which Kazimierz overcame as he gradually made his way from the north to the south of the continent and then back again. He narrowly avoided death on numerous occasions. During his five year journey he met different indigenous inhabitants and learned a great deal about their lives. He fell in love with the natural beauty of the wilderness he saw all around him. His African adventure was superbly recorded by both his writing and photography.

His early life

Kazimierz Nowak was born in 1897 and he was brought up in Poznań, in Poland. At a young age he discovered the pleasure of riding a bicycle, a simple way of getting to know his native land. When older, he worked for an insurance company and during his days off, would take to the road and photograph many of the locations he visited. In 1922 he married Maria and within three years, a daughter and a son had been born. During the Great Depression, Kazimierz lost his job. He then spent many months trying to find employment but to no avail. Needing to support his family, he decided to become a journalist and photographer. He began making journeys across Europe on his cycle, visiting many countries as a foreign correspondent including Hungary, Italy, Belgium, the Netherlands, Romania, Greece and Turkey. In 1928 Kazimierz found himself in North Africa as a reporter covering the war in Libya. It was there, he began to plan his African adventure: to cycle the length of Africa.

His bicycle journey across Africa

In November 1931, Kazimierz travelled from Poland to Naples then crossed the Mediterranean Sea. His plan was to write articles and take pictures en route. These, he would send to Maria, back in Poland, which she would sell to the press. After arriving in the Libyan city of Tripoli, he travelled south into the Sahara Desert riding his well-worn seven-year old bicycle. After many hundreds of kilometres he reached the Oasis of Maradah. There, the Italian authorities couldn't understand how anybody had managed to cycle across the desert – on their own!

Due to the volatile and dangerous region he was about to enter, Kazimierz was ordered back to the Mediterranean. The authorities suggested, if he wished to continue south, it would be safer and easier taking a route further to the east. So, he about turned and went back to the coast, travelling east to Benghazi, then on as far as Alexandria in Egypt. At which point, he then took his bike southwards, following the Nile valley through Egypt, across the

Kazimierz in the desert

Sudan, to the African Great Lakes. It was an area rife with life threatening diseases, including malaria, which Kazimierz unfortunately succumbed to. During this part of his journey, he experienced an attack by a lion and then a leopard and also, by a man wielding a stick!

The terrain he met was extremely challenging, and really, quite unsuitable for cycling. Over more difficult terrain, Kazimierz would resort to simply pushing his bike. His limited possessions for the journey were all strapped to the back, the front and to the cross-bar of his cycle. His bundles included a tent and cooking utensils, along with other personal items such as a toolkit, note books, water container, food supplies, camera and rifle. Kazimierz took to carrying a gun, an essential item to have by his side. He had to be alert to the many potential dangers. Camping alone out in the open with an abundance of African wildlife, he had to be prepared for any encounters. Crossing national borders would

Kazimierz in the Ruwenzori Mountains of East Africa.

often cause problems and could involve days just waiting for visas and other paperwork to be completed. On reaching the eastern Belgium Congo, he walked up into the Ruwenzori Mountains, sometimes referred to as the Mountains of the Moon. He camped at 4,500 metres in the snow, which he realised he had missed. As a Polish man, he was used to seeing snow during many months throughout the year.

Kazimierz was very often hungry, finding it a problem to find enough food as he made his way south across the continent. Despite such challenges, he developed a great affection for the wild beauty he found: '...for a nature lover, the terrors of Africa are not scary at all... the sense of freedom is intoxicating.'

He also wrote: 'In the middle of the boundless savannah I would sleep in a tent feeling completely secure.'

He easily made friends with the different local peoples he met along the way, becoming intrigued by their subsistence and hunting traditions. Using his camera, he was able to take pictures of

Kazimierz enjoyed meeting people along the way.

those he met in local villages, recording their every day lives as they went about their daily business. He managed to trade with people, often picking up food to enable him to continue on his journey. Whenever the opportunity arose, Kazimierz would eat with those he met and talk about their lives. He became fascinated with the indigenous traditions and cultures he encountered. He was eager to understand how so many people managed to survive within an environment which was so very challenging. As he continued pedalling further south, local inhabitants he had visited would alert those ahead, often by the beat of tam-tam drums.

If Kazimierz always enjoyed meeting the indigenous communities he encountered along his route, it wasn't always the case with the majority of white settlements he came across. On such occasions, he often preferred to camp on the outskirts and so avoid any contact. However, he would visit church missions and any Polish farmers he met, often staying with them for a few days, especially if he was having bad bouts of malaria. Others however, including government officials, military groups and hunters, he steered clear of. He generally disagreed with their imperial and exploitative sentiments and their general lack of concern for nature: 'It is true that the Europeans have introduced to Africa the wonders of the twentieth century, but have done so for their own benefit.'

His extraordinary journey had been largely self-funded. However, Kazimierz was provided with free bicycle tyres for his journey from one company in Poland. Fortunately, his plan to support his family by sending articles and numerous photographs back to Maria in Poland, was successful. His reports appeared in both Polish and German newspapers. With his camera, Kazimierz took around 10,000 pictures throughout the entire trip.

Finally in April 1934, he reached the southern tip of South Africa at Cape Agulhas. He had cycled the length of Africa, the first person to have ever done so.

The return journey

Rather than return to Europe by ship, he chose to travel overland but this time, by taking a more westerly route. However, tragedy occurred in the middle of the Kalahari Desert when his battered bicycle finally fell apart. The machine, which had faithfully taken

Kazimierz across Africa and had been patched-up and mended so many times, had a broken axle. It was the final breakage. Fortunately, a local Polish settler provided him with a horse which allowed Kazimierz to travel a further three thousand kilometres. It didn't take Kazimierz long to develop the necessary skills to spend many hours of every day in the saddle. He eventually managed to obtain another cycle from yet more Polish settlers, which took him to Angola. On reaching the River Kassai, Kazimierz decided to continue his journey but by using a locally made dug out

His route through Africa.

canoe. He had no maps of the river, hadn't any experience on how to handle the vessel and on one occasion, faced a serious attack by a hippopotamus.

Unfortunately, whilst negotiating some rapids, his canoe was damaged beyond repair. Having no other transportation available, Kazimierz continued his journey on foot until he was able to purchase another boat. This time, the long narrow boat had a bespoke canopy in the centre which Kazimierz built himself. His river adventures ended at Leopoldville after two months. His long journey along the Lulua, Kasai and Congo rivers had come to an end. On a bicycle once again, he then rode to Lake Chad. There, the authorities of French Equatorial Africa wouldn't allow him to cross the desert by cycle. For safety and practical reasons, it was suggested he join a desert caravan going northward.

So Kazimierz, still wanting to travel independently, bought two camels and hired a herdsman, in short, he formed his own caravan. The camels were to ride upon and to carry any equipment, which including his bicycle. This was another difficult journey where finding enough water and food for his caravan was challenging as it journeyed northward. The next five months was spent crossing the Sahara Desert until he reached the oasis at Ouargla. Kazimierz then continued by cycle for another 1,000 kilometres to Algiers on the Mediterranean coast. As he entered the city in November 1936, he had completed a round journey of some 40,000 kilometres. He had become the first person to travel overland, across the length of Africa and back again.

His return to Poland

Kazimierz spent the last of his money in Algiers buying some warmer clothes as it would be much colder on his return to Europe. He also bought a ticket to cross the Mediterranean to Marseille. Once in France, he headed for the Polish mining community near Etienne. He needed to earn some money to pay for a railway ticket back to Poland. He sold prints of his African trip and took pictures of miners. He then rode to Paris to obtain

Kazimierz with his camel, Ueli

visas for Belgium and Germany.

In December, he arrived back in Poznań in Poland, to the jubilation of family and friends. Over the following months he gave lectures all across the country about his African adventure. His journey had been a success and he began to make tentative plans to cross India and then on into South-East Asia. However, his African journey had taken its toll: his body was exhausted, he suffered frequent bouts of malaria and had developed periostitis in his leg which required surgery. Sadly, whilst in hospital, he contracted pneumonia and died, less than a year after his return home. Kazimierz was forty years of age.

Kazimierz Nowak had completed an altogether amazing journey and a monumental achievement. During his African cycle trip, he had developed a huge affection for the nature and the indigenous peoples he met. His was a truly inspirational adventure.

Richard Halliburton

Who was he?

Richard Halliburton was renowned for his adventurous travels throughout the world during the 1920s and 1930s. He found huge success in sharing his exploits with the public via his many magazine articles, newspaper reports, his lectures and through his popular books. For two decades he completed many unique, daredevil and inspirational challenges in a short life crammed full of adventure.

Early Life

He was born in Brownsville, Tennessee in the United States in 1900. Richard was from a middle-class background, his mother, Nelle Nance was a teacher, his father, Wesley, was a civil engineer and a real estate investor. In 1915, Richard developed a rapid heartbeat for which, he spent many months in bed. Thankfully, his condition steadily improved. In 1917, his brother, who was three years younger than him, died after catching rheumatic fever. His death greatly affected the entire family.

Richard went to Princeton University where he experienced academic success and greatly enjoyed the camaraderie of his fellow students. However, he found himself becoming increasingly restless. For Richard had decided he would become an adventurer and secretly made plans to travel the world. Furthermore, he had worked out that he would be able to make a living as a writer by documenting his experiences. He wrote at the time:

> 'Life is not life if it's just routine, it's only existence and marking time till death comes to divorce us from it all.'

Richard temporarily left university during 1919. Onboard the freighter, *Octorara*, he signed-on as an ordinary seaman bound for London. Richard then journeyed through France and Britain and quickly became enthralled with the excitement of travel. This brief taste of freedom completely convinced him of the life he should lead. So, after his eventual graduation from Princeton, he openly rejected any kind of conventional career, for a life of adventure.

Establishing his dream

In 1921, he began living his dreams. Richard worked his passage across the Atlantic, aboard a ship bound for Europe. He and a companion from university, then made their way to Zermatt in Switzerland where they decided to climb the 4,478 metre high Matterhorn. Neither of them had any previous experience of mountaineering! They managed to find guides to lead them up the mountain in the unusually deep September snows. Having hired appropriate climbing items and with their guides, they began their climb. It was extremely arduous work for such complete novices. But, their guides made sure they were kept safe for the entirety of this iconic climb. After their ordeal their bodies ached having endured such physical toil, but they were both elated with such a monumental achievement.

His friend returned to the United States but Richard made his way through France and Spain. On reaching Gibraltar, as he wandered around the city he decided he would take photographs of certain military installations positioned around the British outpost.

The island authorities were convinced he was a spy whereupon, he was duly arrested and put in jail. Eventually, on paying a fine, he was released and continued on his travels. Throughout the journey, Richard was gathering material for an eventual book. At the same time, he was also writing short articles which he dispatched to magazines back in the United States.

He eventually made his way to India. In Uttar Pradesh he visited the Taj Mahal where he hid at dusk until the area were clear of tourists and the guards had gone home. Then, having the entire place to himself, he swam in the moonlit waters of the grounds. After that, he trekked in the Himalayas then visited Burma and China. While on a boat sailing from Hong Kong to Macao, the vessel was boarded by a band of Chinese pirates and Richard had most of his possessions stolen.

On reaching Japan, he travelled to Mount Fuji where he completed one of the first ever winter ascents of the 3,776 metre high mountain. Similar to his circumstances before the Matterhorn climb, Richard had to acquire both a guide and equipment to take him to the summit. After resting in a hut, part way up the dormant volcano, he and his guide took many hours battling through freezing conditions, blizzards and deep snow to gain the top.

After over a year of travelling, Richard signed-on as a seaman upon a ship sailing across the Pacific Ocean. On his return to the United States he wrote articles and gave lectures about his experiences. He also wrote and had published his first adventure travel book, *The Royal Road to Romance*, which eventually became a best seller.

Further adventures

In 1925 his follow-up trip consisted of a journey through the classic Greek world in the footsteps of Ulysses. It included swimming the 4.5 km Hellespont from Europe to Asia. The swim wasn't easy because of the very strong currents. Although he developed severe cramps, he became the first ever American to complete the swim. He was supported by a friend who followed him in a boat. The swim almost didn't take place after Richard had temporarily been arrested by the Turkish authorities, again being accused of spying. He managed to convince his captors he wasn't taking pictures of nearby military placements, but wanted to have photographs of where he was aiming to swim. After considerable explanation, the swim was allowed. His trip then continued, with an ascent of Mount Olympus in Greece and Mount Etna in Italy.

Returning to the United States he began to write his next book. By now, Richard had achieved a degree of fame. The press were requesting interviews and he had found he was having to give many lectures about his adventures to audiences all across the USA. His original decisions had therefore come to fruition: he had become an adventurer, an author and had achieved enormous success, with his books appearing in the bestseller list!

For Richard's next adventure, he journeyed to Latin America, following the trail of the Spanish conquistador, Hernán Cortés, this time, accompanied by his father, Wesley. Starting from Vera Cruz, the pair along with a guide, walked more than 300 kilometres to Mexico City. The next task was for Richard to climb Mount Popocatépetl, Mexico's most active volcano at 5,426 metres in height. At the summit, Richard needed to take photographs for an article he was being sponsored to write. However, the camera's shutter was jammed so he had to descend the volcano without any pictures. As soon as his father returned to the United States, Richard climbed to the top of Popocatépetl once more in order to take his pictures from the top. Some time later, he went to visit the Maya ruins of Chichén Itzá. Whilst there, he twice dived into the Sacred Cenote, well of sacrifice pool some 27 metres from the cliff-top down into the pool. The first time was in the half light of dusk so he returned the following day to repeat the performance and take pictures.

Richard then made his way to the Panama Canal where he planned to swim its entire length, a total of 77 km! Richard was given permission by the canal authorities as long as he registered himself as a ship and paid the recognised fee for his weight of 140

Richard swimming the length of the Panama Canal, courtesy and copyright Panama Canal Authority.

pounds. The fee amounted to 36 cents! This epic challenge was fraught with danger including the possibility of being attacked by barracudas and alligators for which a sharpshooter was required to follow in an escort boat. The swim had other dangers including having a cocktail of potential killer diseases living within the water.

Sunburn was a huge problem, with Richard developing numerous blisters along with suffering from dehydration. Another nuisance was the occasional sewage discharges out of giant ocean liners passing by as he swam. And, there were the massive and highly dangerous currents to contend with around all the large locks along the canal's length. As well as having a rifleman inside the escort craft, there was also a photographer, a newspaper reporter and one of Richard's friends as a companion. The boat-crew bore witness to this historical event which was, a complete success. Richard Halliburton became the first person to swim the entire length of the Panama Canal including swimming through

223

the colossal locks. The swim took nine days with a total of 50 hours having been spent in the water.

On his way back to the United States, Richard visited the Inca centre of Machu Piccu in Peru and travelled to Buenos Aires in Argentina. Whilst in that city he bought a trained monkey and an old hurdy-gurdy and went off to perform around the streets. Unfortunately, when the authorities found he didn't have the necessary licence, they were displeased, for which Richard spent a night in a city jail. Again!

The latest batch of adventures had provided material for many articles, a whole host of lectures all over the country, and of course, another book. By now, Richard had reached celebrity status across the United States. He began mixing with other well known figures including certain Hollywood personalities. It was around this time he began a secret relationship with Paul Mooney at a time when being gay was generally considered unacceptable throughout society and what's more, illegal.

For his follow-up adventure, Richard decided he would visit various regions of the world, in his own light aircraft. In 1921 he bought a bi-plane and he and Moye Stephens, a pilot, decided to fly to a variety of obscure locations in their small scarlet and gold plane. They named it *The Flying Carpet*. After detaching the wings and shipping the aircraft to Europe, their journey could begin. Their travels started by flying across the Sahara where they spent two weeks with the French Foreign Legionnaires in the desert. Then, in the Middle East, Richard decided he would swim across the Sea of Galilee. In doing so, his sunburn was so severe, he needed to spend several days in hospital.

On reaching India, the authorities there, gave the pair permission to fly to Mount Everest. Their bi-plane's maximum flight height was officially just over 4,800 metres. However, by stripping all the heavy items out of the plane, they calculated they would be able to fly even higher in the thin air. But, it did mean flying without parachutes, tools, anything heavy and flying with only a part load of fuel. It worked and they flew up to around

5,400 metres. However, at their maximum height, in front of Mount Everest, Richard almost fell out of the bi-plane after unbuckling his safety belt so he could stand-up in the cockpit to obtain better pictures. Due to the drag he had created, the plane suddenly stalled! The aircraft took a nose-dive for over 300 metres before Moye was able to stabilise it. However, Richard did manage to take the first ever aerial photographs of the highest mountain in the world. They went on to visit remote regions of south-east Asia before their return to the United States. During their 18 months of flying, they had covered over 54,000 kilometres and visited 34 countries.

Back in the United Staes, Richard resumed his lecture tour, with new material, began writing his new *Flying Carpet* book as well as setting-up home with Paul Mooney. Feeling restless again, Richard decided his next series of adventures would involve travelling to various locations around the world and then write about the people and events he experienced along the way. His publishers simply gave him a free-hand to find interesting items to write about. For part of this journey, Richard planned to follow in the footsteps of Hannibal, by riding aloft an elephant up to the Great St Bernard Pass in the Alps. The elephant in question was named Dally and was kept in Paris. It took time to train the elephant because the creature was scared of cars passing her. So, whilst the necessary elephant training was being carried-out, Richard travelled afar, not wanting to waste any time. This included a journey to Russia where he interviewed the assassin of Czar Nicholas II, and, also included an attempt to sneak into the holy city of Mecca.

Returning to France, Richard was pleased to find a much improved Dally. The elephant had now learnt how to walk alongside passing cars without panicking. From Martigny in Switzerland, Richard and Dally took three days to make their way up to the monastery on the St. Bernard Pass. All along the route, there were large numbers of spectators wanting to witness the event. At the 2,469 metre high pass, as well as fifteen local monks from the monastery, there were around two thousand other people. They were all gathered to see a man upon an elephant arriving, just as Hannibal had done so long ago. However, on the way back down the mountain, Dally bolted after a company of mountain soldiers had fired a cannon volley in their honour!

Richard in the footsteps of Hannibal.

The final adventure

In 1938 Richard travelled to Hong Kong where he had a Chinese junk made which would be capable of sailing across the Pacific Ocean. The plan was for the junk to reach the Golden Gate Bridge for the opening of the 1939 San Francisco Golden Gate International Exposition. After failing to procure a suitable vessel in Hong Kong for the proposed journey, Richard decided that a Chinese junk would need to be built entirely from scratch. Finding the many experienced people to skilfully construct such a craft wasn't easy. Eventually, a junk was built which was named *Sea Dragon*.

With Richard and a crew of ten, including his partner Paul, they sailed out of Hong Kong harbour. However, on experiencing bad weather, structural problems with the junk, along with crew injury and illness, the *Sea Dragon* was forced to return to Hong

Kong. After modifications to the vessel were made and members of the crew recovered, they set sail once again on 4 March. Radio contact was made at regular intervals up to 23 March 1939, when a radio message from the junk's captain reported they were encountering a typhoon near to the International Dateline: 'Southerly gale. Rain squalls. High sea… Having a wonderful time. Wish you were here instead of me.'

It was the last contact the *Sea Dragon* ever made to the outside world. The junk was never seen again. The event came as a massive shock to many people across the world who had become dedicated fans of Richard Halliburton and his many extraordinary adventures.

It was the end of his incredible life which had been lived to the full. Of a man, who was forever chasing a new dream and then sharing it with thousands of followers by his lectures and through his writing. Richard had once written about the dangers of his adventurous lifestyle he led:

> And when my time comes to die, I'll be able to die happy, for I will have done and seen and heard and experienced all the joy, pain and thrills – any emotion that any human ever had – and I'll be especially happy if I am spared a… common death bed.

For whatever reason, the stories of this American adventurer have largely been forgotten. His books are still available and can be enjoyed by all those wishing to lose themselves in a variety of 1920s or 1930s derring-do escapades. Richard Halliburton was the complete adventurer.

Felice Benuzzi

Who was he?

Felice Benuzzi was an Italian mountaineer, diplomat and writer. He is famous for his audacious escape from a British prisoner of war camp in Kenya during World War Two. After escaping with two others, they climbing Mount Kenya and then broke back into prison! Their adventure succeeded against incredible odds and all because Felice simply loved the look of the mountain!

Felice Benuzzi, courtesy and copyright Family Benuzzi Archive.

Early Life

Felice was born in Vienna in 1910. His mother was Austrian and father was Italian. In 1918, the family moved to Trieste in northeastern Italy. At a young age, Felice developed a passion for the mountains and visited the Julian Alps, the Dolomites and the Western Alps where he climbed with his father and friends. He went on to study law in Rome where he graduated in 1934. As well as his academic studies, between the years 1933-35, Felice represented Italy as an international swimmer where he took part in numerous competitions.

In 1938, he joined the Italian Colonial Service and was sent to Addis Ababa in Abysinnia where he worked for the Government of Italian East Africa. He married his wife, Stefania, in the same year. In 1941 Allied troops overran the Italian forces in East

Africa, as a consequence, Felice became a prisoner of war. Stefania and Daniela, their young daughter, eventually managed to return to Italy while Felice was eventually transported to British POW Camp 345, very close to Mount Kenya.

Mount Kenya

The camp was situated just outside the small town of Nanyuki, in the middle of Kenya and almost directly on the equator. Felice and the other new inmates had arrived during the rainy season. From their POW barrack, there was no view to be had outside, apart from that of continual mist and cloud. Felice knew the geography of his new location and was eagerly waiting to catch a glimpse of his first ever, 5,000 metre mountain. As the rain fell and the low cloud remained, he began to get impatient. But then, whilst dozing in his bunk early one morning, he was woken-up. His fellow prisoner pleaded: 'Quick. Get up. Come and look at Mount Kenya... Hurry up or the peak will be covered with clouds again!'

Felice wrote:

> ...and then I saw it. An ethereal mountain emerging from a tossing sea of clouds... a massive blue-black tooth of sheer rock, inlaid with azure glaciers; austere yet floating fairy-like on the horizon... I stood gazing until the vision disappeared among the shifting cloud banks... I had definitely fallen in love.

Being a prisoner of war in such a remote African location was depressing for the prisoners. Any attempt of escape appeared to be futile: neutral Portuguese Mozambique, was over 2,000 kilometres away, he hadn't any of the necessary documentation, no money or maps and couldn't speak fluent enough English. And, then there were those vast tracts of wild countryside with its many dangerous creatures to deal with. Escaping to Mozambique, just wasn't a realistic option.

However, the acute tedium of internment had quite suddenly been eased for Felice on seeing Mount Kenya for the first time.

As a great admirer of mountains, the view had stirred his thoughts and emotions. He gradually developed a daring scheme to break free, to scale the peak, and then, break back into the prison. To be free on top of the mountain – never before had the cliché about 'why climb a mountain' been so pertinent: 'because it's there!' His mind was both daunted and excited as to how he could possibly attempt such an impossible and altogether crazy plan.

*They had no map, just a wrapper from a
cold meat tin to guide them!*

He began to think how it could be done and how he might acquire and adapt a range of items needed for the climb. There were so many things to consider. There were so many unknowns and few places where information about the mountain might be gleaned. What would it be like in the thin air on top? How could he make crampons, ice-axes and find suitable ropes to climb with? He would need to have warm clothing and a great deal of food. He didn't have a map or any kind of written climbing guide for Mount Kenya.

How would they escape from the camp, and then return? What

wild creatures might there be on the way? The floodgates of thought had been breached, it was difficult to think of anything else. Felice confided in and enlisted the help of Dr Giuàn Balletto, who had had some mountaineering experience. Gradually, as they talked the logistics over, the numerous problems about the proposal, just might be solvable.

First of all, Felice wrote to his family for boots and warm clothing, which hopefully would arrive as a POW parcel. After acquiring two hammers and befriending the camp blacksmith, two rudimentary ice-axes were made. Crampons were created from pieces of discarded metal and barbed wire, and sisal cord from bunk-beds made a usable climbing rope. Extra clothing was fashioned from blankets and they accumulated as much extra rationing as they could from other prisoners. They were still unclear of the route they should take to the summit. However, after receiving new Kenylon tinned meat rations, their problem was partially solved because upon the tin was an image of Mount Kenya! This one sketch would help guide them up the mountain. Needless to say, favours were called-in from other inmates, especially those involved in various prison-camp workshops. As well as Giuàn, a third person was asked to join them: Enzo Barsotti, who had no experience at all of climbing mountains but was very enthusiastic about their breakout. When all the extra clothing, food supplies and equipment were finally gathered, it was time to begin this extraordinary expedition.

So, on 24 January 1943, they began. Immediately outside the barracks, where prisoners grew vegetables in gardens, food stocks and equipment for their trip had been secretly buried. They then hid in the gardens until after dark before it became possible for the three prisoners to escape. Having made a replica key, the trio unlocked the door in the garden fence and made their way across open country, thorn scrub and grassland. They needed to lie low as a train and military vehicles crossed a railway line and a road along the way. Fortunately, the sky was clear and the snows on the summit of Mount Kenya, informed them they were going in the right direction.

They moved as quickly as they could, and after four hours, they had reached the edge of the forest which encircled the entire East African mountain. They journeyed with care as they moved through the forest trying, at all costs, to avoid any sign of human activity. After some time, they found a river flowing down the mountainside. By its fast flowing waters, they then trekked, in the knowledge that, if followed, it would eventually lead them to the top of Mount Kenya. That night, they believed they were far enough away from human habitation, so they pitched their tent and lit a camp-fire. In their dawn slumbers, they were aware of rustling amongst the trees. On challenging the noise they witnessed the disappearance of a leopard! Later on in the day, they also had to avoid a nearby rhinoceros.

Around all East African mountains are zones of vegetation which change as a person travels higher; the next zone the Italians met was of bamboo. It was slow work trying to make any progress because their rucksacks were continually being caught by strands of bamboo. As they rested in a clearing within the undergrowth by the waters of the stream they were following, another creature appeared. It was a solitary bull elephant. They entered another zone of vegetation growth, of giant lobelias and groundsel which were as high as trees. As they travelled higher Felice's two companions developed fevers and they were all suffering from the cold. At around 4,000 metres they made their base camp where Enzo remained due to his worsening condition.

Felice and Giuàn went off to view Batian close-up, to decide how the highest of Mount Kenya's summits might be climbed. They returned and prepared for the climb the following day. On the 4th February, they arose and had a meagre breakfast, consisting of two biscuits each, a drink of Ovaltine, powdered milk and sugar. For any climbers wanting to ascend challenging peaks at high altitude, this just wasn't enough. But, with their diminishing food supplies, it would have to do. At 2 am, they then left camp to make an ascent of Batian.

Mount Kenya.

It took the two men four hours to get to the bottom of the rock face. They then began climbing the very steep, icy and technically testing route. For the two mountaineers, it felt good to be climbing, using all four limbs. However, care had to be taken as many of the holds were filled with snow and ice. The difficult climbing was made more challenging as a storm began to develop, bringing with it lowering cloud, strong winds and heavy snow. They were having problems feeling their fingers because of the extreme cold. Reluctantly, they took the decision to retreat. By 5 pm they were again at the bottom of the face and by 9 pm, they were back at base camp.

After resting, they returned to climb Point Lenana, another of the three main peaks, at 4,985 metres. As well as being slightly lower than Batian, it was also a less testing peak to climb. Even though they were in an even greater weakened state, they arrived at the summit. This time, they achieved success! Their names were placed in a bottle which was then carefully left between rocks, after which, they raised an Italian flag. Later, Felice wrote:

> …After advancing a few yards along the broad shoulder we saw the cairn marking the top not far from us… A great peace hung over the broad expanse. Under the dark velvety sky the wonderful scenery of the country at our feet had a strange radiance. This was the climax of eight months' preparation and of two weeks of toil. It was worth both… Yes, we were delighted to be on Lenana… It was time to hoist the flag.

They then dumped any access weight from their rucksacks, including their hand-made rope and crafted crampons. They both felt incredibly tired, exceedingly hungry but at the same time elated in having climbed their mountain. As with the climb on Batian, it didn't take long for the mist to close in and the snow to begin. Floundering with fatigue, they gradually made their way back to the tent.

After their success, the three Italians retraced their steps back down the mountainside and consumed their remaining scraps of food. They followed the same river downhill, which, in their mental haze and extreme hunger, appeared to take less time. For their final three days of freedom, they had no food. They just walked and walked. And so, after eighteen days on Mount Kenya, they broke back into POW Camp 345. With their replica key, they went through the gate which they had escaped from. The next morning, they happily reported to the British Compound Officer: 'Good morning!' they said together. Each was sentenced to 28 days close confinement which was reduced to seven because the Camp Commandant 'appreciated their sporting effort'!

On the 20 February, a Kenyan newspaper reported that when a group of Britains had been on Mount Kenya, they had seen an Italian flag flying at the summit of Point Lenana. The headline read: 'ESCAPED ITALIAN PRISONERS FLED TO MOUNT KENYA' This revelation soon became international news. As a consequence, because of such unwanted exposure, the three mountaineers were moved to a more secure camp far away from Mount Kenya.

Felice on the summit of Mount Ortler in the Italian Alps in 1929, courtesy and copyright Family Benuzzi Archive.

Life after the war

After the war Felice became a diplomat and worked in a variety of locations around the world. His professional life was varied and he was faced with a number of challenges. With positions from vice consul to consul general, he held posts in Paris, Brisbane, Karachi, Canberra and Berlin. In 1958, during his time in Canberra, a second child was born into the family, a girl they named Silvia. When Felice and his family were in Germany, it was at the height of the Cold War. From 1973-76 Felice was promoted, and served as the Italian Ambassador in Montevideo in Uruguay. His diplomatic skills were such that he also became involved in talks to settle the disputed Tyrol region of the Alps. He was also part of an international delegation putting together the new Antarctic Treaty.

Felice's passion for the mountains continued and, whenever possible, he would go off into their heights. Wherever he was posted around the world, he took advantage of exploring the nearest high peaks. He made a number of ascents of mountains in Australia, New Zealand, Bolivia and Mexico. He also climbed Kilimanjaro in Tanzania and, at the age of 72, Mount Whitney in the USA. Felice wrote many articles and some books about a range of subjects which included mountains and mountaineers. He was also a founding member of the mountain environmental organisation, Mountain Wilderness.

Felice Benuzzi died in Rome, in July 1988. His unbelievable story of escaping from a World War Two POW camp, climbing Mount Kenya and then breaking back into prison, is now legendary. It is a story about a proud Italian and of a mountain man who dared to follow his dream of standing upon a beautiful peak. In his honour, the col between Point Dutton and the Petite Gendarme has been named the 'Benuzzi Col'. A part of the mountain Felice once fell in love with, will forever be linked to his name.

Emma 'Grandma' Gatewood

Who was she?

In 1955, Emma Gatewood became the first woman to walk the 3,000 kilometre Appalachian Trail in the United States in one complete hike. Before this date, her life had been one of hard labour, of bringing-up a large family and running a farm. Unfortunately, she had been subjected to years of abuse from a violent husband. For most, such a life would have taken its toll, but at the age of 67, Emma decided to take-on a long-distance hiking challenge.

Emma Gatewood on the Webster Cliff Trail, courtesy and copyright Marjorie Gilliam Wood

Her earlier life

Emma had been brought-up in a rural family of fifteen in the state of Ohio. In 1907, at the age of nineteen, she married Perry Gatewood. They moved onto a tobacco farm where, like many others during this time, it became a constant challenge to make a living. Their lives were difficult with a continual string of daily farming chores to work through. As well as farm labouring, Emma also managed to bring-up eleven children.

Every minute of every day, she was hard at work. Unfortunately, throughout her marriage, Perry physically abused his wife. There were some occasions when Emma was almost beaten to death. Over the years she had numerous bones and teeth broken along with a catalogue of other injuries inflicted upon her. Emma's screams were loud enough for all to hear, both children and neighbours. To escape, she would often run off into the woods to find solace amongst the trees. Fortunately, after decades of continual violence, she managed to gain a divorce, which was almost unheard of in 1940.

Freedom!

Years later, after her children had all left home and she was no longer living on a farm with her abusive husband, Emma picked up a magazine. It was a copy of the *National Geographic*, in which, an article about the Appalachian Trail, caught Emma's attention. It described a newly created hiking trail crossing a total of fourteen states in the east of the nation. With route descriptions

and photographs, the feature described this new trail as being a 'straightforward walk'. Reading further, she learnt that, so far, no female had yet completed the trail.

There and then, Emma decided she would be the first. There was something about the report which just sparked her imagination. She had lived her entire life in a rural setting, so was used to both the outdoors and labouring hard for many hours at a time. Being rid of her husband and with all her children having flown the nest, there was nothing holding her back. It was an opportunity to

Emma walking the Oregon Trail in 1959, courtesy and copyright Marjorie Gilliam Wood.

do something noteworthy: 'If those men can do it, I can do it'.

Emma's training involved a daily routine of increased walking near to her home, eventually getting up to sixteen kilometres per day. She saved as much as she could from her job working at a nursing home. And, she kept her intensions from her family to avoid any fuss.

She eventually made her way to the Appalachian Trail to begin her walk. Emma carried just one change of clothing stuffed into a homemade denim bag which she draped across one shoulder. She had a blanket, a raincoat and a plastic shower curtain to shelter under. For sustenance she carried some dried beef, cheese, nuts and ate edible plants she found along the way. She wore sneaker shoes but had no sleeping bag, tent, compass or map! Emma, mother of eleven children and grandmother of 23 grandchildren, carrying her burden across her shoulder of some fifteen kilograms, was ready!

Emma on Wildcat Mountain, New Hampshire, courtesy and copyright Marjorie Gilliam Wood.

Starting from the northern end of the trail was a harsh introduction to her long-distance hike. The trail was very steep and after a few days she became lost due to the paths being unclear and because she had broken her spectacles – without them, she couldn't see! Emma was eventually rescued by rangers who were out looking for her. Their suggestion was that she should go back home. However, she treated the experience as just a set-back. She wasn't going to be put off because the following year, at the age of 67, Emma returned.

For her second attempt, Emma started from the southern end of the trail. This time around, she definitely had more success. Although many sections were straightforward to hike, other parts had poor route markings and were sometimes overgrown. Emma

Emma at South Edgemont, Massachusetts, courtesy and copyright Marjorie Gilliam Wood.

Emma hiking in Pennsylvania, courtesy and copyright Marjorie Gilliam Wood.

chatted to local people she came across along the way who often provided her with directions. Many she met were extremely kind and offered her shelter and a meal for the night. She stayed in a variety of places on her long trek including huts, farm buildings, on front porch swings, in gardens or upon a bed of leaves beneath the trees.

On some occasions, she needed supplies so would make her way to nearby stores. At other times she might be offered lifts to towns some distance away to purchase items. However, she only accepted if she was then returned back to the same point on the trail. During her days walking, Emma discovered it was invariably

241

easier going uphill than down. As she continued further, her leg became painful, which, along with the bunions upon her feet, made walking increasingly challenging.

Walking the trail required her to be constantly alert to any potential problems. As well as having to concentrate on her route finding, there was always the threat of meeting a venomous rattlesnake or copperhead snake. On one occasion, she was confronted by a bear, which she had no problem in seeing off! However, there was a host of less threatening creatures for Emma to glimpse, including deer, beavers, chipmunks, raccoons and an array of birds from doves to eagles. As a lover of the natural world, Emma took great delight in simply walking amidst nature, day after day.

As she ventured ever northward, people began to talk about the old lady who was walking the trail. It wasn't long before local newspaper reporters went out to find and interview Emma, or 'Grandma Gatewood' as she became known. They wanted to know why a 67-year-old grandmother was tackling such a challenging walk. 'I thought it would be a nice lark' or 'because I wanted to' were very often her replies. Emma didn't tell people that it was a chance to try and free herself of all the years of domestic violence she had been subjected to.

She continued to make her way along the trail but unfortunately, there was an increase in extreme weather conditions. At one section along her route, after a period of severe storms, she was faced with a raging flooded river. Fortunately, she managed to cross the river with the assistance of two teenagers who were out walking the trail. The youngsters roped up, with Emma in the middle, and they then waded chest deep in the fast current in order to gain the other side. She found the last section of the Appalachian Trail particularly tricky because of its steep terrain. However, she finally completed her long trek on reaching Mount Katahdin in Maine on 25 September 1955. It had been a tough experience and had taken her 146 days. Speaking to somebody when she had finished the trail she said, 'I would never have started this trip if I had known how tough it was, but I couldn't and I wouldn't quit.'

Through sheer grit she had become the first female to walk the entire length of the Appalachian Trail in one continuous hike!

Celebrity status and further walks

Emma's fame quickly spread: news of 'Grandma Gatewood' completing her walk appeared in national newspapers and she was interviewed on television. In 1960 she walked the trail once again in one continuous trek, becoming the first person to complete the journey twice. In 1963 at the age of 75, she walked it for a third time but this time in sections. Emma also hiked other long-distance routes including the 3200 kilometre Oregon Trail from Missouri to Oregon which took her 95 days. She had truly become a long distance hiker.

Emma at Mount Mansfield, Vermont Long Trail, courtesy and copyright Marjorie Gilliam Wood.

Emma's reports of how parts of the Appalachian Trail had not been looked after, helped bring about improvements and for a greater care of the trail. Many say, her involvement saved the trail: it had given it prominence which, in turn, led to better maintenance and a gradual increase in its use.

Emma Gatewood died in 1973, after living an extremely eventful life, some of which we could describe as being quite horrendous, other parts, exceedingly celebratory. Her story illustrates to us all, that we are never too old to both have and fulfil a dream.

'If you want to do something you should do it and not wait for someone to tell you that you can do it' her granddaughter, Marjorie Wood, once remarked.

By completing a number of long distance hiking trails, Emma Gatewood had become an extraordinary woman of adventure. She is, quite simply, an inspiration to us all.

Bibliography
and further reading

Here is a list of sources where extra information might be found about each of the adventurers within this book.

Edward Whymper

Triumph and Tragedy the Life of Edward Whymper, Emil Henry
Scrambles Amongst the Alps, Edward Whymper
Travels Amongst the Great Andes, of the Equator, Edward Whymper

Isabella Bird

This Great Beyond, Cicely Palser Havely
A Curious Life for a Lady, Pat Barr
Travels with Isabella Bird, film by National Library of Scotland
'Isabella Bird', BBC Radio 4, *Great Lives*

Edward Payson Weston

A Man in a Hurry, N. Harris, H. Harris and P. Marshall

Lucy Walker

Women Climbers: 200 Years of Achievement, Bill Birkett and Bill Peas-cod
Articles about Lucy Walker (online)

Thomas Stevens

Around the World on a Bicycle, Vols. 1 and 2, Thomas Stevens
Through Russia on a Mustang, Thomas Stevens

John Muir

My First Summer in Sierra, John Muir
The Wild Muir, edited by Lee Stetson
A Passion For Nature: The Life of John Muir, Donald Worster
'The Sierra Club', the US environmental organisation, founded by John

Muir (online)
Matthais Zurbriggen
From the Alps to the Andes: Being the Autobiography of a Mountain Guide, Matthias Zurbriggen, translated by Mary Alice Vialls

Annie 'Londonderry' Kopchovsky
Around the World on Two Wheels, Peter Zheutlin
Song: *'The Ballad of Annie Kopchovsky'* by Evalyn Parry

Mary Kingsley
Travels in West Africa, Mary Kingsley
'Mary Kingsley' BBC Radio 4, *Great Lives*

Édouard Alfred Martel
Édouard Alfred Martel, Yorkshire Ramblers Club Journal (online)
Padirac: Its History and a short Description, Édouard Alfred Martel
Contact the British Caving Library (online) They have extensive information about all aspects of caving, including Édouard Alfred Martel

Fanny Bullock Workman
Peaks and Glaciers of Nun Kun, Fanny Bullock Workman
Two Summers in the Ice-Wilds of Eastern Karakoram, Fanny Bullock Workman
Algerian Memories, Fanny Bullock Workman

Fridtjof Nansen
Nansen, Roland Huntford
Farthest North, Fridtjof Nansen
Contact the Fram Museum in Oslo, which has extensive information about Fridtjof Nansen (online)

Annie Smith Peck
A Woman's Place Is at the Top, Hannah Kimberley
In Search for the Apex of America: High Mountain Climbing in Peru and Bolivia, Annie Smith Peck

Matthew Henson
A Negro Explorer at the North Pole, Matthew Henson
To the End of the Earth, Tom Avery

Dumitru Dan
Contact the Buzau County Museum which has a comprehensive collection of Dumitru Dan's artifacts and information about his walk around the world (online)

Freda du Faur
The Conquest of Mount Cook and Other Climbs, Freda du Faur
Between Heaven and Earth: The Life of a Mountaineer, Freda du Faur 1882-1935, Sally Irwin

Nobu Shirase
1912: The Year the World Discovered Antarctica, Chris Turney
Search for articles about the first Japanese Antarctic Expedition (online)

Harriet Chalmers Adams
Harriet Chalmers Adams: Adventurer and Explorer, Durlynn Anema
Harriet Chalmers Adams: The original Adventure-lebrity (online)

Geoffrey Winthrop Young
Geoffrey Winthrop Young, Alan Hankinson
Mountain Craft, Geoffrey Winthrop Young
On High Hills, Geoffrey Winthrop Young

Millican Dalton
Millican Dalton: In Search of Romance and Freedom, Matthew Entwistle

Gleb Travin
Search for translated articles about Gleb Travin (online)

Kazimierz Nowak
Across the Dark Continent: Bicycle Diaries from Africa 1931-36, Kazimierz Nowak

Richard Halliburton
American Daredevil - The Extraordinary Life of Richard Halliburton, the World's First Celebrity Travel Writer, Cathryn J Price
The Royal Road to Romance, Richard Halliburton
The Glorious Adventure, Richard Halliburton
New Worlds to Conquer, Richard Halliburton
The Flying Carpet, Richard Halliburton

Felice Benuzzi

No Picnic on Mount Kenya, Felice Benuzzi
The Heart And The Abyss - the Life of Felice Benuzzi, Rory Steel

Emma 'Grandma' Gatewood

Grandma Gatewood's Walk, Ben Montgomery
Film, Eden Valley Enterprises (online)